X AGENDAS FOR ARCHITECTURE —

X AGENDAS FOR ARCHITECTURE —

Marc Schoonderbeek
Oscar Rommens
Loed Stolte
eds

Artifice
books on architecture

CONTENTS —

INTRODUCTION TO X AGENDAS FOR ARCHITECTURE —
ASCERTAINMENT, INVITATION, RESPONSES

Marc Schoonderbeek,
Oscar Rommens,
Loed Stolte

> Vagueness is a form of tolerance that produces a diversity of architectural languages, each inscribed on the particularities of a border condition.
>
> S Umberto Barbieri, "Preface", *Border Conditions*

ASCERTAINMENT

The first decade of the twenty-first century saw the emergence of a **wide variety of understandings of space** in a wide variety of disciplines. During that decade, an impressive array of highly specific understandings of space were developed, influenced by scientific, social, ideological, economic and political changes and debates, and, in most cases, made evident via the altered experiences of space itself, either from an individual or a collective perspective. Ironically, our 'global planet', which necessitates the dissolving of boundaries, has been stifled by the tendentious reflexes that nation states have shown in implementing stricter spatial exclusions. During this period, interest in the conflict of space and **the space of conflict** emerged from various moments of crisis that have had a global impact – among them economic stagnation, financial crises and environmental devastation – combined with the "Clash of Civilisations" ensuing from 9/11. Each of these events has contributed to the climate of in(st)ability and insecurity that exists in current architectural discourse. The prevailing atmosphere of a discipline that meanders from crisis to crisis has typified architecture during this period.

Yet the current shaky ground beneath the discipline of architecture is neither necessarily conceived nor treated as problematic since many of its practitioners seem to recognise the teeming potential implicit in this period of uncertainty. In architectural discourse, the evident material fatigue of the welfare state (and all the apparently related areas of crisis) are countered by alternative forms of engagement, be it through technological exploration, new practices of spatial appropriation or social engagement. Environmental concerns and the impending collapse of the capitalist market economy have led to a general shift towards sustainable architectural strategies of reuse, preservation and regeneration. The sense of crisis has set in motion a wide-ranging exploration of architecture's knowledge, means and ends.

A superficial reading of such developments in architecture as a discipline would probably focus on the growing emphasis on techniques rather than discourse as a symptom of architecture's inaptitude. Whether at the level of design methodologies, digital technologies, material and structural possibilities, or the instruments of sustainability, architectural professionalism today either seems to ignore, or is simply indifferent to the **cultural significance** of architecture. What appear to remain at present are the kinds of operative practices that confirm the economic **servitude** of architecture (as design). This servitude in turn surrenders to philosophers and thinkers the difficult task of contemplating the complexities and meanings of territorial occupation, and to the politicians (and their business interests), decisions on spatial demarcation.

However, in the European context in particular, given the issues of nationality and religion that have become central within recent political discussions, this reading of current developments in architectural discourse deserves further articulation. Ideological and political debates have had little influence on architectural discourse, unlike those typical of the 1930s and 1980s. These were the decades when ideological agendas were regarded as an intrinsic part of architectural discourse and explored the boundaries of the discipline with a burst of energy with regard to the potential of architectural experimentation. At present, the search for the **space of encounter** that architecture is supposed to offer is in need of renewed and intensified theorisation, framing and straightforward acknowledgement. With the previous remarks in mind, it has become disenchantingly clear that contemporary provocations cannot extend their ideological intent by finding a common ground in architectural discourse. These strategies clearly do not work today. Thus, in contrast to the subversive aesthetics-based strategies of the historical avant-gardes and the 'alternative' tendencies during the 1980s, any counter-position today has to deal with the process of institutionalisation in order to avoid dispersal, irrelevance or simply non-existence.

INVITATION

In autumn 2011, the Delft University of Technology architecture research group, Border Conditions & Territories, organised the symposium and lecture series "X Agendas for Architecture", during which a number of architects, theoreticians and scholars gave presentations of their work. The symposium reflected on the themes formulated in the research group's first publication (the 2010 book *Border Conditions*), which contains a comprehensive overview of the group's architectural research and design projects. Additionally, the lecture series focused on four themes that were considered relevant for current architectural and scholarly practices (namely "Aesthetics of Sustainable Architecture", "Territories of Drawing", "History, Collective Memory and Politics" and "Experimentation in Architectural Design"). In both the symposium and the lecture series, attempts were made to frame and discuss these areas of development in light of tendencies in the contemporary discourse, and to consider the necessity of a new **architectural agenda** for future action. The diversity of the questions discussed all evolved around the presumed challenges the architectural community faced in a shared future of architecture. In attempting to gain insight into the specificity of contemporary knowledge, the tools and tasks of architecture were discussed, focusing on issues of time, space and matter (with the respective concomitant notions of spatiality, temporality and social being), circumnavigated by radicalism and pragmatism, experimentation and conventionality.

During the symposium, the notion of the border was further elaborated upon as an alternative, future model for positioning the architect *vis-à-vis* current developments in society and globalisation. Following the somewhat conventional and increasingly irrelevant distinction between radicalism and pragmatism, which was discussed in terms of the dichotomy between avant-garde versus mainstream architecture, "**border thinking**" was proposed as a third conceptual model, one in which the architect is no longer considered a heroic master nor a servant to the powers in force, but rather as being situated in the margins of a border condition itself, and finding relevance or legitimacy through this in-between position. Through border thinking, one would no longer be bound by dichotomies, but be able to contemplate interrelationships on all fronts. This fluctuating position simultaneously offers the possibility of addressing the wide variety of conceptual understandings of space, as well as opening previously unimagined perspectives.

Furthermore, any attempt to construct an agenda cannot abstain from outlining discursive trajectories in order for architects to decide on their position by tracing historical developments. The key historical proposition in this context would seem to be as follows: after the period of deconstruction in architecture, during which an inexhaustible array of **different forms of fragmentation** were introduced, which resulted in a process of testing the limits, knowledge and tools of the discipline by 'infecting' it with other disciplines (in an effort to move away from the rediscovery of architecture's autonomy during Postmodernism), and after a period of design-oriented experiments within an increasingly global urban field, during which the deliria emanating from 'reality' tended to determine, rather than inform, architectural projects, the last decade has seen the emergence of an interest in considering the possibility of a renewed **synthetic approach** to architecture.

Perhaps one could say that the process of continued fragmentation had previously resulted in a withdrawal reflex. The 'bigger questions', if one can at least interpret these as attempts towards "synthesis", have been deemed suspect for several decades, ever since Jean-François Lyotard's dismissal of the "grand narratives" within the postmodern condition. Thus, avoiding larger hypotheses, the absence of an all-encompassing agenda is indicative of the continuous withdrawal of architecture into fragmentation (as if, tautologically, to self-fulfil its own prophecy). Of course, the point currently would not be to re-establish a synthetic whole, an epistemological construction in which everything is rationally ordered into a coherent entity. Rather, a synthesis should be attempted that takes fragmentation as the very basis of its hypothetical constructions. An **amalgam** needs to emerge that connects and integrates the characteristics (and scale) of the fragments rather than suppressing them in order to strengthen the larger whole. In this attempt to frame and discuss the current developments in architectural discourse at large, and extend the questions relating to the necessity of architectural agendas, we decided to expand the range of invited authors and combine the symposium line-up and related lecture series with a selected group of recently appointed deans at architectural faculties worldwide, a development that seemed to us to be part of a transition towards a new generation of agenda-makers in architectural education.[1]

1. In alphabetical order: Balint Bachmann, Sigrún Birgisdóttir, Martin Chenot, **Marcos Cruz**, Lene Dammans Lund, Evin Douglas, Ana Duarte Lanna, Hugo Dworzak, **Manuel Gausa**, **Urs Hirschberg**, Sebnem Hoskara, Johannes Käferstein, Peter Kjaer, Karin Laglas, **Sarah Lorenzen**, Qingyun Ma, Sacha Menz, José Manoel Morales Sanchez, **José María Wilford Nava Townsend**, Torben Nielsen, Lu Pinjing, **Christopher Platt**, Monica Ponce de Leon, **Javier Quintana**, Hannah Le Roux, Wang Shu, Marianne Skjulhaug, Richard Sommer, Bob Somol, Lars-Hendrik Stahl, Sally Stewart, **Toomas Tammis**, Zhu Wenyi, Sarah Whiting, Alexander Wright, Alejandro Zaera-Polo and Weimin Zhuang.

RESPONSES

Javier Quintana insists on a market-oriented education system that offers room for scholarly initiatives, operates within a network of professional entities (whether offices, corporations and/or institutes), and addresses architecture as a combination of artistic craft and entrepreneurial expertise.

Gijs Wallis de Vries utilises the work of Giambattista Piranesi to offer six arguments that refocus architecture's attention towards the essential characteristic of the "*città pensile*", namely the timeless imaginative construction of desire rather than the necessity implied by temporary norms.

Marc Koehler calls for a complete reorientation of the architectural field by arguing for the architect's role as initiator in current building practices, and claims this should have consequences for architectural education as well.

Sang Lee theorises the surface condition as an all-encompassing understanding of the built environment, in which surfaces constitute structure, skin and interiority, thus sketching an interrelational model of space.

Alexander Wright underlines the importance of education and foresees a much-needed new direction in architecture, one that actively contributes to current professional developments and multi-disciplinary innovations in both architectural design and architectural research practices.

Manuel Gausa's 15-point celebration of architecture embraces forms of diversity and complexity, turning contemporary design and research practices into architectural laboratories that focus on the exploration of dynamic sets of informational space-time relations.

Urs Hirschberg is convinced that the future of architecture lies completely in the development of rigorous research programmes that will help clarify how architecture can solve actual problems. As a consequence, education should aim at developing creative generalists rather than experts.

Patrik Schumacher pleads for a new, broader movement in architecture, namely "parametricism", which is an information-rich interface of communication, resulting in a built environment that is a complex matrix of territorial nuances.

Christopher Platt upgrades the classical role of the architect as *homo universalis* within the era of globalisation, and argues for the education of architects as professionals who are able and equipped to offer unique spatial identities in the current, not very symmetrically ordered world.

Gerard van Zeijl offers a short historical overview of the discursive developments in architecture from the perspective of theory, and retraces the paradoxical nature of the discipline, forever caught in the pendulum movement between thinking in images and objectifying thoughts.

Alejandro Zaera-Polo traces the archetypes of architectural education in order to propose a new educational model for the future. He calls for a refocus on the productivity and operability of the architectural discipline and redefines the architecture school as a laboratory for practical solutions.

Martine De Maeseneer carefully describes the working method of her own practice by clarifying the importance she places on the play of associations between words and spatial concepts as the basis for architectural design.

Leonel Moura presents his artistic experiments in which creative machines play a determining role. In the artistic processes Moura designs, the role of human creativity is minimised and machines become active agents in the production of unexpected artistic work.

Malkit Shoshan criticises taxonomical thinking derived from the Enlightenment and calls for the model of biotopic thinking as a way to spatially organise the world of things, life and culture.

Weimin Zhuang introduces the notion of fuzzy logic in architecture. He claims that decision-making in the architectural profession has had considerable difficulty in coming to terms with the numerous complexities of current architectural practice, which fuzzy decision-making is able to cope with.

Sarah Lorenzen explains the consequences that occur when architectural education is opened up to minorities, claiming that 'professionalism' and 'good design' are aspects of the contemporary architectural discipline that need to be enhanced and cherished, without necessarily surrendering to dogma and fixed certainties.

Michiel Riedijk composes his autobiographical agenda as a trajectory of personal experience, disappointments and insights over time, while simultaneously offering definitions of, and future expectations for, the architectural profession.

Marcos Cruz raises a number of issues deemed important for contemporary architectural education, proposing that 'lateral design' should be at the core of the curriculum: longer-term programmes with more specialised and experimental education, located in work environments that are innovative and stimulate a continuous, in-depth exploration of the possibilities of materialised ideas.

Pnina Avidar traces the historical changes in terminology in architectural discourse of the last century, and asks for the emergence of a new terminology that can embody the expanded and diversified condition in which the profession nowadays operates.

Henriette Bier discusses the changed status of the work of art and architecture in the age of digital reproduction and observes that both authorship and practical implementation have now evolved from object-oriented experimentation into interactive human/non-human agency.

François Roche reflects on the differences between Paris and Bangkok, and places his bet on the current energies to be found in Bangkok, which originate from the tension between two urban realities, namely the city as the culmination of capital, and the city as infinite improvisation.

Toomas Tammis argues for the case-specificity of experimental tactical design and research practices as the proper way to operate within contemporary architectural fields, where further professional fragmentation coincides with the increased complexity of architectural objects.

Machiel Spaan believes navigating the architect's diverse fields of operation is an aspect of the architectural profession that is not only rather underestimated but currently also highly relevant, allowing the architect to simultaneously probe the potential of observation and imagination.

Hannah Le Roux sketches the conditions of architectural education in an extreme societal condition of inequality, and argues for an appreciation of the three main conditions that have emerged: the rich versus the poor, and the middle, which is committed to bridging these.

José María Wilford Nava Townsend believes that architecture serves the communities for which it is built and should provide its inhabitants and/or users with the hope of a better life. The sustainability in architecture Nava Townsend seeks essentially means the critical understanding of the fabrication of a 'home'.

Micha de Haas departs from his professional mid-life crisis in order to arrive at the insight that the role of the architect is in need of new forms of engagement, namely the ability to manoeuvre in open processes and negotiate qualities into design, thus allowing for the disappearance of personalised authorship. ▼

A REFLECTION FROM OUTSIDE THE CAGE —

Javier Quintana

We cannot change if we keep doing the same.

Albert Einstein

1. THE NEED FOR CHANGE

The situation for architects has changed during the last decade. Compared to the end of the twentieth century, when we were still considered trendsetters and almost media stars, we have lost credibility and have become more vulnerable and isolated. This is not a personal conviction but the reading of an accumulation of circumstances that are affecting the future of our professionals.

It is clear, for example, that society is demanding the transformation of our cities into more human environments. But it is also obvious that architects, as opposed to environmentalists or planners, are not leading this process.[1] At the same time, it is worrisome to see how we have disappeared from the lists of the most desirable professions.[2] And while we are finally adapting to the new design technologies, we still find it very difficult to apply them to the construction phase. Compared to other professionals, we have become less relevant, less seductive, more vulnerable, and incapable of leading through innovation.

This state of affairs represents a serious problem, but, as an educator, it is even more of a concern to see how very few schools of architecture are addressing the situation. Most of these issues have educational implications that very few institutions are willing to assume. It seems as though schools have somehow become self-centred, caged spaces without much interaction with reality.

This became evident to me during the 2nd International Architectural Education Summit (IAES) on "Innovation in Architectural Education", held in Madrid and Segovia in 2011, when a group of "alternative platforms of education" (galleries, institutes, web-based groups) justified their success on the failure of other, more established institutions to meet the demands of the market.[3] A more positive message emerged from the 3rd IAES Summit, held in September 2013 in Berlin, when a few schools showed how they are departing from their traditional base. Nevertheless, the question remains, how representative is this group?[4]

From my point of view, the heart of the problem lies in the restrictive vision we architects have of our own discipline. As a result, schools have been overlooking the complexity of the construction process, reacting to very few of its needs, and failing to acknowledge the role of some of its protagonists. As a consequence, our programmes do not reflect sufficient diversity, our faculty members lack cross-disciplinary experience, and our student profile is too homogeneous.

The gap between the academic and the professional side of our discipline is another part of the problem. If, for instance, we acknowledge that the construction sector represents more than 15 per cent of the GDP in civilised countries, it is surprising to discover that the sum of all graduate programmes in architecture represents less than one per cent of the business of education.[5] This means we are educating merely the tip of the iceberg, leaving the rest outside our sphere of influence.

1. Urban ideology has shifted from a design focus towards environmental and sociological concern, leaving architects in the background of the discussion. See Burdett, R, and Philip Rode, "The Urban Age Project", in *The Endless City*, London/New York: Phaidon, 2007.

2. According to *Fast Company, Smartplanet* and *Business Week*, architects have disappeared from the 25 first positions of most wanted jobs, falling even lower than 40th place. See also the *Bureau of Labour Statistics' 2006–2007–2008 Occupational Outlook Handbook*.

3. The alternative platforms were Aedes Network Campus Berlin; The Why Factory, Delft; and BIArch: Barcelona Institute of Architecture.

4. The self-centred attitude also became obvious in November 2011 at the Old School/New School ACSA Conference in Hollywood, where US administrators brainstormed about the future of architectural education as an internal issue and not as a response to society. It was equally worrisome at the 14th Meeting of the European Network of Heads of Schools of Architecture held in Chania, Greece, 2011, when, under the title "Doing More with Less: Architectural Education in Challenging Times", most of the discussions were focused on how to survive financially rather than questioning the model that had brought schools to this situation.

5. The information refers to the US and UK market at the Master's degree level. See *Graduate Enrolment and Business Report, 1999/2009*, Washington: US Bureau of Economic Analysis, 2009.

In a similar way, if we survey the academic portfolio of schools, it is shocking to realise the scarcity of educational options for mature professionals, or how the entrepreneurial and managerial aspects of our profession—the ones that could make us stronger in times like this—are completely overlooked. [6]

2. OPENING THE CAGE

It seems that all these circumstances are affecting not only the conception of our schools but also their relationship with the world outside. Maybe it was not our intention, but we have built 'academic cages' that were conceived as permeable, but which are ultimately very difficult to penetrate.

As the founding Dean of the IE School of Architecture and Design—an international educational initiative created by the IE Business School—I have tried to use innovation and an integrated vision of our discipline to open these cages. [7] Experience has taught me that once you leave the cage, reality's influence is much stronger, and interaction with other disciplines becomes easier.

Through innovation, I mean to challenge the traditional academic content of our studies, update the way we distribute knowledge, and reconsider student and faculty member profiles. Put simply, we have tried to redefine what we teach, how we teach it, and whom we target.

At the IE School of Architecture and Design, we identified entrepreneurship and the intersection between design and management as the key tools for providing a competitive answer in the present context. This was reinforced by the conviction that given the number of architects running their own practices, entrepreneurial management has to be part of our curriculum. [8] At the same time, we decided that our programmes should be delivered in a 'blended' format, allowing our students to work while they study. We also invited people from financial institutions, city halls and NGOs to be part of our student and faculty body. Even though they are not architectural institutions, they are urban related and key participants in the construction process.

The translation of this philosophy into the school has been wide and varied. For example, we designed an undergraduate programme in which, from the first year on, students are taught presentation, negotiation and marketing skills. At the same time, we used IE's expertise in online learning to create an internship programme that allows students to work part-time at first-class international practices, and to accumulate two years of professional experience by the end of their degree. [9]

More recently, IE accredited a post-professional Master's degree course in Architectural Management and Design, which aims to fill the gap between design and management in the education of architects. The programme addresses "the business implications of design decisions", and combines face-to-face periods with distant learning. As the first of its kind, the programme has attracted students from more than 20 nations and includes faculty from the world's most prestigious practices. [10]

The school has also launched a Master's degree course in Workspace Design, and explored other shorter formats in collaboration with top schools in different countries. For a young initiative such as ours, this has been the perfect way to gain international visibility and acquire experience outside the traditional realm. As a result of this course, architecture in our school has been revealed to students through the eyes of academics and professionals from more than fifteen disciplines. Using their expertise, we have been able to provide a cross-disciplinary approach to our studies and open the cage to new players in our field.

Finally, in partnership with the IE Business School, we have created design-oriented courses for non-architects where our teachers have interacted

6. In the United States, only Harvard University and the University of Southern California are making meaningful efforts to develop an executive education division for architects.

7. Based in Madrid, IE Business School is a top ranking, higher education institution focused on entrepreneurship (#1 in Europe according to the *Financial Times* ranking, November 2013). For further information see http://www.ie.edu. On IE University and IE School of Architecture and Design visit http://www.ie.edu/university and http://www.ie.edu/architecture.

8. Visit http://www.ie.edu. With regard to the number of self-employed architects, see the UIA's 2005 report on *Architectural Practice Around the World*, p 53.

9. IE has been ranked #1 in the world a number of times for its online programmes. See, for example, "Distance-Learning Special: 2010 Special. Which MBA?" published by *The Economist*, or the *Financial Times* 2014 rankings for MBA online programmes.

10. Lecturers and instructors include top individuals from OMA, Snøhetta, BIG, Foster and Partners, SOM, David Chipperfield Architects, Zaha Hadid, Gensler, Rogers Stirk Harbour and AEDAS. For further information, please visit http://www.mamd.ie.edu.

with future managers, forcing them to readapt the discourse and expand architecture beyond its usual grounds. An example of this is the "Think-Design Workshop" series included in IE's international MBA, in which students are required to redefine the space they work in, both at school and at home. At a more junior level, this happens through the so-called "Experimentation Workshops", where instructors from adjacent disciplines teach our undergraduates in fields such as film, illustration or architectural writing.

Another interesting area for cross-disciplinary interaction has been our Architecture Venture Lab. Through interaction with advisors from different fields, students are required to develop a business proposal related to architectural design. It has been striking to see how half the students either proposed radical departures from the traditional concept of an architectural practice, or alternative ways of becoming an architect.

I very much like all these initiatives since they provide an opportunity for us to understand architecture beyond the vision of architects.

3. CONVICTIONS

In addition to the academic implications of these initiatives, my years as Dean at IE have taught me that given the complexity of the contemporary situation in relation to the creation of a school of architecture, there are some factors I consider crucial:

First of all, schools have to be market oriented but also student and scholar centred. If we do not succeed in listening to the latter's needs, we will not be able the deliver the right infrastructure for their success.

I also believe that the construction of a school of architecture has to be driven by external forces as well as internal ones. In other words, it is critical to have an intellectual or academic agenda, but at the same time we have to listen to what society and our professionals demand. [11]

Furthermore, schools should not only reflect the vocational component of designers, but also incorporate the spirit of entrepreneurs. According to UIA statistics, more than 50 per cent of architects end up starting a firm at some point during their careers, so it is essential to provide the right training to ensure their success. [12]

It is common to identify the periphery or so-called "border" condition as the one that allows vagueness and diversity. But when thinking about how our school was conceptualised six years ago, I prefer to use the idea of being off-centre to envisage the place that IE occupies. It is this territory that IE believes holds the most interesting opportunities for new agendas, and, unless institutional inertia changes, the only place where real innovation can be achieved.

Although this is certainly a peripheral location, and one that sometimes involves isolation and risk, given the present state of architectural education, it is also, in my modest opinion, the most interesting place to be.

11. On this subject, see Iñiguez de Onzoño, S, *The Learning Curve. How Business Schools are Transforming the World of Education*, Madrid/London: IE Publications, 2011. See UIA's 2005 report on *Architectural Practice Around the World*.

12. In the case of the United States, the figures speak for themselves: there are more than 102,000 registered architects compared with 36,300 students. See UIA's web page http://www.uia-architectes.org. The data was taken from the section "Architectural Profession Around the World".

Javier Quintana is the Dean of the IE School of Architecture and Design, an innovative educational initiative created by the top ranked IE Business School, offering blended programmes in Spain and the UK. Quintana is promoting a professionally oriented model of education based on an entrepreneurial spirit, the merge of design and management and the use of innovation. Quintana holds a Master's degree from Columbia University and has a PhD from the University of Navarre. He is also founding partner of Taller Basico de Arquitectura SLP, an experimental practice focused on design innovation and architecture culture. His work has been awarded, published and exhibited both nationally and internationally. www.ie.edu/architecture, www.tallerbasico.es.

SIX THESES AFTER PIRANESI —

Gijs Wallis de Vries

INTRODUCTION

Architectural theory today is concerned with many issues related to things outside architecture, such as sustainability, heritage or the global city. Since the expression of these contents in architecture is disappointingly unable to liberate spatial uses and experiences that meet enlightened ecological, cultural or political criteria, and since the profession and even education are lending their ears (and eyes) to marketable trends, while following state of the art building technology and digital technology, it is time for architectural theory to address its future autonomy. I would like to take this occasion to clarify this future autonomy in six points, for which I have borrowed the headings from the eighteenth-century architect and engraver Giambattista Piranesi.

1. AUT CUM HOC/ AUT IN HOC
Either with this, or in that.

Piranesi, Giambattista, *Osservazioni sopra la Lettre (...)*, 1765, frontispiece.

The problem of architectural theory is the character of its discourse. Often the adequacy of its architectural facts and spatial practices is taken as a criterion to judge the value and relevance of the discourse, or an insurmountable opposition is assumed to exist between language and image. The real problem is presence and representation; that is, the inscription in architectural discourse, visual or verbal, of both the object and the subject of space. This reciprocity constitutes Piranesi's famous manipulation of perspective that tricks the viewer into entering the imaginary space of his drawings and 'touching' the objects in it. A disjunctive synthesis (*cum/in*), rather than a false dilemma (*aut/aut*), is the message of this etching and its confrontation between verbal and visual discourse: the writing *with* a pen on matters of architecture, and the writing *in* architecture itself as a material fact.

2. RERUMQUE NOVATRIX/ EX ALIIS ALIAS REDDIT NATURA/ FIGURAS

And nature, innovator of things, makes from one figure another.

Ovidius, *Metamorphoses*, XV

Piranesi, Giambattista,
Parere su l'architettura,
1765, plate 7.

How to innovate? Design is a form of imagination, invention and fiction. Taking into account the necessity to confront and study architectural traditions, treatises and theories as well as urban facts and existing spaces, design must operate change. So, how to make change? Quoting from Ovid's *Metamorphoses*, Piranesi uses the word "figure". A figure is more than a form. The statement is not about natural evolution, nor is it suggesting an analogy of technical or stylistic change with nature. The crux is the encounter between matter and thought, produced by literal (architectural) and figural (linguistic) turns.

3. NOVITATEM MEAM CONTEMNUNT/ EGO ILLORUM IGNAVIAM

They despise my novelty, I despise their cowardice.

Sallustius, Iugurtha

Piranesi, Giambattista, *Parere su l'architettura*, 1765, plate 9.

The cowardice of design is the eagerness to please the client. The courage of design is the creation of the unexpected: a novelty that is not intended to satisfy the arrogance of the architect or the branding of his name, but a novelty that is inspired by a desire of space. Modernity has always claimed novelty and Piranesi has indeed been mentioned among the first moderns. The concept of novelty is tied up with technical rationality, spatial functionality and creative originality. Therefore, the problem is the "ego", a problem of identity ("self" and "other"), of reason and doubt ("cogito"), and of being and becoming. It addresses my desire, regardless of whether I am producer or consumer. How to educate the ego? To overcome cowardice (fashion, convention, the state of the art) an ethical theory of architecture is required.

4. AEQUUM EST VOS COGNOSCERE/ QUAE VETERES FACTITARTUNT/ ATQUE IGNOSCERE/ SI FACTITARUNT NOVI

It is just that you know what the ancients have done, and that you ignore it if the young are creating things.

Terentius, *Eunuchus*, Prologue

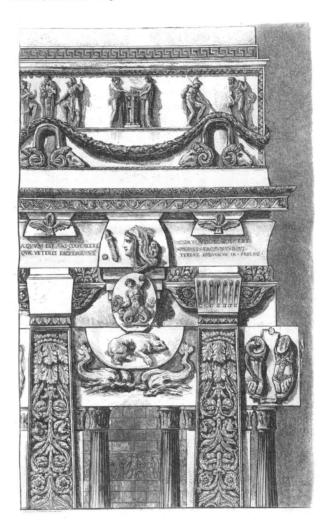

Piranesi, Giambattista,
Parere su l'architettura,
1765, plate 5.

      The problem that Piranesi addressed in his time was that of classicism. According to him it was not about teaching the standard and imitating it, but discovering the exception and emulating it. In the statement above, quoted from the Roman playwright Terence, the word "and" that juxtaposes respect and disrespect produces an interesting turn in the 'quarrel' between the ancients and the moderns by celebrating the will to match precedents and celebrate the infinite variations, which Piranesi himself found in antiquity itself, and for which he praised Mannerism and the Baroque. After Postmodernism, deconstructivism and other Modernisms, the challenge is to forever emulate exceptions, classical and other.

5. POUR NE PAS FAIRE DE CET ART SUBLIME/ UN VIL MÉTIER OÙ L'ON NE FEROIT/ QUE COPIER SANS CHOIX

In order not to make this sublime art into a routine craft in which one would only copy without choice.

Le Roy

Piranesi, Giambattista, *Parere su l'architettura*, 1765, plate 8.

For architecture today, the problem of history is to deal with heritage (classical, modern, colonial, industrial, religious, military, etc). Reusing is not about preservation but about use. It is about identity, both respect for it, and its novel interpretation. Identity is empirically given, however. To understand it, it must be conceptualised. One of the tasks of architectural theory is to critique prevailing opinions of identity. The critique of local and vernacular identity must explore otherness and exteriority: the fears and desires that make its horizon.

6. PER L'UTILE, PER LA PERMANENZA E PER LO STUPORE

For utility, for permanence and for amazement.

Piranesi, *Emissario del Lago Albano*

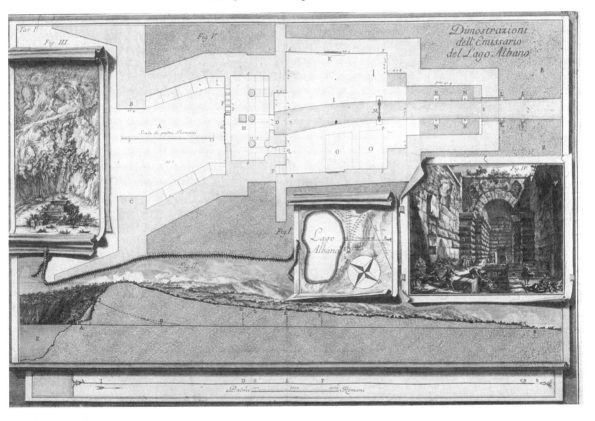

Piranesi, Giambattista, *Emissario del Lago Albano*, 1762, plate 1.

Piranesi presented his reconstruction of ancient Rome as *Città Pensile*. This "hanging city" consists of "pensile architecture" and "navigable infrastructure" – the full quote is: "città pensile e navigabile al di sotto". In late modern terms it may be conceptualised as an archipelago city with dense, strong enclaves and informal, open space in between. Documenting the grounded solidity and public utility of aqueducts, sewers, roads, bridges, foundations, walls and vaults, Piranesi also presents a heavenly city that offers myriad escapes: from tumult to serenity, from traffic and business to strolling and lingering. Drawing amazing flight lines, Piranesi maps the Campo Marzio as a configuration of intricate spaces and cosmic places. Thus the *Città Pensile* honours our desire for escape, not with suburban sprawl, but with sanctuaries, theatres, stadiums, arcades and gardens. The architecture is indeed "amazing", a word that translates *stupore* and connotes the figure of the labyrinth ("maze"). Today escape is still, and surely even more, a challenge for architecture. Instead of condemning it and all the shopping malls, food courts, gated communities and holiday resorts that satisfy it, it is better to grasp its *desires*, its moves and its imaginations, rather than redirecting architecture to so-called *needs* and the societal, political, economical, cultural and ecological *norms* that are supposed to fulfil them, it is time to think of the *longings* that make cities desirable.

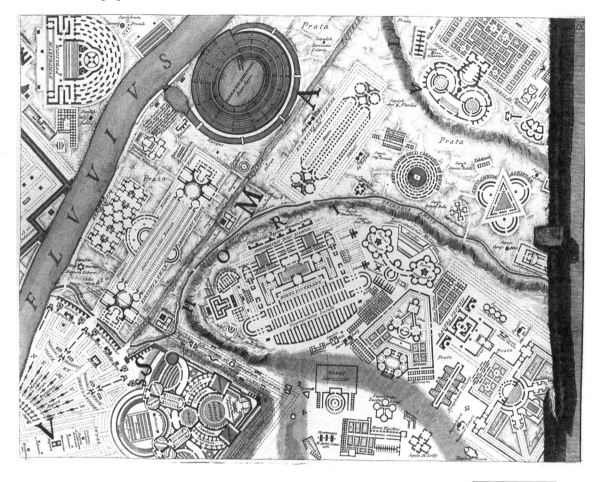

Gijs Wallis de Vries is Associate Professor at the Faculty of the Built Environment of the Technical University of Eindhoven and teaches architectural history, theory and design. In 2014, he published *Archescape – On the Tracks of Piranesi*, a book that analyses Piranesi's vision of the Campo Marzio as 'Città Pensile' in the light of Deleuze's concept of the flight line. Gijs has published in a wide variety of books and journals (*Archis*, *OASE*, *Topos*, etc) and participates in conferences regularly. In 1990, he obtained his PhD with *Piranesi and the Idea of the Magnificent City*, Amsterdam: 1001 Publishers. ▼

Piranesi, Giambattista, *Il Campo Marzio dell'antica Roma*, 1762, icnografia, plate 9.

THE NEW ARCHITECT —

Marc Koehler

English interpreter, Laura Vroomen

In recent decades the graduate programmes offered by Dutch architectural institutions have become both more specialised and fragmented. The degrees at the Faculty of Architecture and the Built Environment at Delft University of Technology, which include Real Estate and Housing, Building Management, Building Technology, Architecture, Urbanism and Landscape Architecture, follow completely separate tracks. Each direction features a miscellany of graduate seminars with little or no cooperation between them. There is hardly any synergy or dialogue between the various specialisations.

This is not an isolated case. On the contrary, it reflects the fragmentation of the current building chain. The age in which we live, founded on a neoliberal economic model, stimulates the hyper-differentiation of goods and services and gives rise to an increasingly fragmented building sector with a new power structure that excludes the architect.

Having been marginalised in recent decades, the architect is now merely a small link in a complex chain of advisors and managers who support the project developer. As a result, part of the architect's traditional role as primary advisor to the client and user has also been taken over by others. The architect is no longer one of the driving forces behind a project and has lost much of his or her influence regarding its quality. An informed debate about the built environment is primarily taking place on the sidelines.

The neoliberal model is hierarchical and works top-down, with each level trying to pass risks down to the level below, which in turn has to find ways of safeguarding itself. The result is a rise in cumulative costs. And with building now far too expensive, all parties end up playing it safe. The current situation is inimical to creativity and innovation.

At the top of the chain we find the financiers – the banks and investors lending their money to developers and housing corporations that enter into fixed-price agreements with their preferred partners, such as contractors who, in turn, make agreements with their subcontractors, manufacturers and product suppliers. The developer is supported by an army of advisors, from engineering consultants to quantity surveyor, from PR and marketing agency to real estate agent. Only when the financial, functional and planning frameworks have been set out in a development model does the architect come into the picture, called upon to inject some character into the model for a meagre fee. As a "designer", his impact on the building is limited to the facade zone, often no more than about 30 cm deep. The result is superficial skin-deep architecture. Literally.

The neoliberal model has also marginalised the user. The resident – "the consumers" – are only involved when virtually everything has already been decided. At best, they can choose from a few predictable layout variants and kitchen types, but has no real say on the dwelling's plan, finishing or character. Therefore, it should come as no surprise that projects from this period – from around the turn of the century until the present day – are vacant and no longer sell.

Yet there is no reason for pessimism. The recent economic crisis has blown big holes in the neoliberal model. Now that no money is being lent, traditional developing parties are having a timeout, which is creating opportunities for enterprising (groups of) private individuals (self-builders, building groups) and architects to reinvent the development process and initiate their own projects. The property market is changing rapidly: whereas it used to revolve around supply generated from the top down, it is now more and more about the demand and self-directed actions of the user (formerly the residential consumer). And this user is becoming increasingly knowledgeable about building and more likely to adopt the role of self-builder or initiator. This change is coupled with growing pains, however. Institutions whose dominance within the construction chain was taken for granted until recently – from banks and estate agents to developers and corporations, from government to university, and from the BNA (Royal Institute of Dutch Architects) to the NAi (Netherlands Architecture Institute) – have now lost ground and need to reinvent themselves. What used to be imposed from the top down will now have to be done in consultation with the user.

This situation offers a new generation of architects the chance to explore new territory. Not through opposition or escaping into nostalgia, theoretical abstractions or utopian projects, but by entering the market with innovative ideas, services and products, and a balanced business plan. In this way the architect becomes the initiator and stimulator of self-created opportunities to renew the building chain and the property market.

It is not easy to capitalise on this opportunity. It will only happen if architects collaborate and learn more about the specialist areas on which the quality of their work has come to depend – those of the financiers, developers, builders and marketing experts. The architect cannot do everything; they are more of a mediator, linking networks and bringing stakeholders together in enduring building coalitions. These coalitions consist of small entrepreneurs who co-develop a product as joint owners, bearing the risks and responsibilities together. This enables the architect to realise better buildings at lower costs. Forming *the* link between the private client and these building coalitions, the architect has to be a multi-disciplinary, creative entrepreneur, a spider in the web in 2016.

The architects of the future are concept developers, developing new products and services they can apply more than once, in order to be able to evaluate and optimise them. This will reduce the cost of building and make quality more affordable. Like the design of a chair or car, it is not just the idea and the first impression of the design that counts, but above all its lasting functional value and long-term emotional value. The feasibility, durability and effectiveness of a design are all becoming more important. The investment in satisfied customers will trump short-term profit. To achieve this, the architect will have to enter into long-term relationships with co-creators, such as builders and material manufacturers, and assume control within the building chain by taking the initiative.

The development of innovative buildings requires intensive knowledge development. For this, the new architect must engage in ongoing empirical research into the lifestyle and culture of users, into new technological opportunities, and into economic models for the funding of ideas. At the same time, architects must carry out design-based research into the opportunities offered by (new) locations for new buildings, transformations or additions. They will use advanced software to support the work and thought processes and will be constantly using new media to communicate with various parties.

The problem is that architecture degrees are too one-sided. Students are not really taught the practice and business side of things that would allow them to set up as independent, all-round entrepreneurs, nor do they learn the skills of collaboration or how to form new alliances or corporations with the other disciplines in the building chain. This makes their position fragile.

This brings me back to an earlier point: are the academies and universities sufficiently aware of the need for a pro-active and integrated approach to architecture, where collaboration, entrepreneurship and an understanding of practical issues are integral parts of the design and analytical process? It is high time for institutions to develop degree programmes in which concrete links are established between Real Estate and Housing, and Building Technology and Architecture. A joint venture with the Department of Industrial Design (ID) is a logical next step: branding, marketing, entrepreneurship, R&D and product development have long been integral parts of the ID degree. Right across the board, architectural education needs to pay more attention to day-to-day professional practice by hiring lecturers for their professional performance alongside the usual academics. Collaboration with companies (for work placements) is crucial here. Needless to say, such a new direction will have to go hand in hand with the necessary scientific reflection.

Times are changing. And universities will have to change, too, in order to give birth to a new generation of civil engineers and architects; a generation that will jointly develop innovative products and refuse to be enslaved by project developers or banks. It is up to these pioneers to build the new economy.

Of course, the chances of this new architect being a success depend on many factors. The biggest risk for architects as mediator is that they will try to do and know everything instead of being a spider in the web. When architects try to control the whole process alone, they leave little room for others to contribute. While collaborating, the architect must leave room for others to develop and fully cultivate their talents. If not, the architect may end up isolated again. It is crucial that architects enter into an enduring relationship with specialists, manufacturers and financial advisors they trust and are willing to accommodate in this partnership. The art of "mediating" is all about jointly realising your own dream and vision as well as those of your partners.

Finally, it remains to be seen whether all parties will retreat to their old positions as soon as the economy picks up again, rather than continuing to work intensively on creating new opportunities together. The integrated partnership we now have could well disappear once more. While this crisis lasts, we should make the most of it for experimentation, networking and creating partnerships, so that when the economy improves, the foundations that were laid will remain firmly in place.

An important question to ask here is how developers in particular will position themselves when the economy recovers. Will they work with architects and other pioneers on an equal footing, investing as co-creators in innovative and risky projects? Or will they retreat to their old, familiar positions without taking the risks needed to explore new markets?

Marc Koehler is the Director of Marc Koehler Architects, which he founded in 2005. As a creative engine, his studio is a dynamic, collaborative design and developing agency, working across a diverse range of themes, including product design, private housing, co-op development and educational buildings. With a user-centred approach, Marc's studio acts as a mediator in the diversified field of the architect.

———————

SURFACE AND MIMESIS —

Sang Lee

The analytic philosopher Avrum Stroll posits that the so-called "Leonardo surface", named after Leonardo da Vinci, is not material but abstraction.[1] It not only separates but also binds together two different entities and states. The surface as abstraction is also an interface. It is an ontological plane with no "divisible bulk" shared between two given substances.[2] It also indexes fluctuations of influences or forces. Conceived as a Leonardo surface, the architectural envelope becomes a *surface-objectile,* an agent that both demarcates and conflates.[3] The assemblage of the architectural envelope is dynamic and indexical. Thus, the architectural envelope not only reflects the external variations and use of resources, but also the internal conditions. The envelope promotes a certain kind of equilibrium through mediation and interface.

Surface conditions contribute crucially to our understanding of our *Umwelt*[4] in an ecological manner.[5] The envelope as ecological surface provides an immaterial or minimally material presence, an interface between the interior and the exterior, a membrane that separates and connects, and a nexus between the artificial and the natural. We conceive of an ecology through *invariants* that inscribe our place in the physical environment, and *affordances* that allow us to identify with the ecology in a sensuous way.

Frequently expressed in instrumental and functional terms, the notion of mimesis, often "biomimesis", is considered in architecture as serving our necessities, needs, comfort, pleasure and desire. Such a conception misplaces the fundamental role of architecture as mediation, both sensorial and environmental. By valorising functionality, we refer to mimesis of nature as an approach to *solving* our problems. It is also appropriated to commodify desire and emotion. This view lacks critical and renovative discourse by focusing narrowly on solving our problems that stem from environmental human excesses. In the name of sustainability, we stuff our Junkspace with more junk and try to avoid the nagging, guilty feeling that we are ultimately committing suicide in the process.[6] Instead of confronting the pathology directly, we install mechanical devices to prop up and replace failing organs. Such contrived mechanical organs satisfy our excesses and reinforce our dysfunctional so-called lifestyle. As Slavoj Žižek entertains, it is "the ultimate perverse vision" of the human body as a collection of organs "as in those unique utopian moments of hard-core pornography" in which the body is "thus transformed into a multitude of 'organs without a body', machines of *jouissance*...."[7]

Mimesis should serve instead to interrogate our relationship with natural organisms and nature at large. The prevailing notion of mimetic architecture advances yet another version of the hegemonic natural history which extends the man-against-nature confrontation. It is intent on how to mitigate our problems, and on how to make our life more convenient and entertaining by fetishising the organs deprived of the body. Such mimesis only reinforces how we can exploit nature and subjugate it to the human-centric world view. The so-called biomimetic architecture comprises nothing but teleological exercises that ultimately would not contribute to a sustainable condition. It indicates that mimesis is a way of replicating an ideal. However, this view presents a rather mechanical construct without the projective, creative and generative capacities of mimesis as empathy.

Walter Benjamin once indicated mimesis as the production of empathetic similarity in both sensuous and non-sensuous ways.[8] Mimesis consists

1. Stroll, Avrum, *Surfaces*, Minneapolis: University of Minnesota Press, 1988, pp 40–46.

2. Stroll, *Surfaces*, pp 40–46.

3. Deleuze, Gilles, "The Fold", *Yale French Studies*, no 80, Baroque Topographies: Literature/History/Philosophy, Jonathan Strauss trans, New Haven, CT: Yale University Press, 1991, pp 227–247.

4. According to Jakob von Uexküll, *Umwelt* indicates a subject-specific conception of the world. Each respective species has its own meaningful *Umwelt* to which it is tuned. See note 13 to the right.

5. Gibson's *ecology* consists of *invariants*: those that provide constant reference, such as the horizon or the regularity of the paving pattern of a sidewalk, and *affordances*, our understanding and recognition as to what we can do with objects in situations around us. Furthermore, Gibson's theory rejects the discrepancy between appearance and actuality; on the contrary, the sense of actual space is derived from the configuration of surfaces.

6. Koolhaas, Rem, "Junkspace", *October*, 100, 2002, pp 175–190.

7. Žižek, Slavoj, *Organs without Bodies: Deleuze and Consequences*, London: Routledge, 2004, pp 172–173. (Emphasis in original).

8. Benjamin, Walter, "On the Mimetic Faculty", in *Reflections: Essays, Aphorisms, Autobiographical Writings*, Peter Demetz ed, New York: Schocken Books, 1978, pp 333–336.

of both recognising and producing similarities. It is a capacity to connect with the surrounding ecologies. In mimesis, the subject and the object entangle and exchange places. The sensuous similarity indicates the subject's body and its direct, unmediated imitation of the other. The non-sensuous similarity is mediated by speculation. The latter is produced by *agency* (eg literature, painting, music, dance, architecture, etc) through media. It may not involve actual objects. In Benjamin's mimesis, environmental affinities replace the conquest-exploitation approach. They "dissolve the contours of the subject/object dichotomy into reciprocity and the possibility of reconciliation".[9] In such mimesis, the surface is not an iconic abstraction mediated by signification, but an index of *poiesis* in the Aristotelian sense.

In another instance – Derrida's reading of Aristotle's *Poetics* – mimesis takes place in an intrinsic relationship with the way nature (*physis*) unfolds itself: "*physis* includes its own exteriorisation and its *double*. In this sense, then, *mimesis* is a 'natural' movement."[10] Mimesis also produces metaphors, the non-sensuous similarity through language. Yet another view arises from the Subject-Self duality of the human mind, which consists of the conscious and the subliminal.[11] In this Subject-Self conflation, mimesis is a projective, modulating empathy between the Subject and the Self. To attain such empathy, we project ourselves onto someone and/or something, and imagine them in our body. The imaginative projection and empathy form "transcendence", which ventures beyond the Subject-Self construct.[12] Yet such transcendence depends on the body: the imaginative projection is autonomic. It draws on the exchanges between the perceiving Subject and the observed object, together forming empathy.

What we find in common in the preceding notions of mimesis is an indexical medi(t)ation that is porous and permeable. In this sense, mimesis is a membrane and a surface through which the subject and the object exchange shared values and empathetic affinities. The surface-index of subject-object becomes intermodal and transcendent, participating in the operations of *physis*. Mimesis provides for architecture a specific and concise view of surface as the medi(t)ator of the unfolding of nature, subject and self. It is the architecture of the intermodality between subjectivity and its environmental contingencies. Being mimetic is about how we situate ourselves and establish an intimate relationship with the self-emerging natural environment. Common in the aesthetic evaluation of architecture is the assessment of geometrical harmony, proportion, symmetry and order, with respect to the prevailing *dispositifs*.

The various notions of mimesis suggest in common that mimesis consists in developing affinities and empathetic exchanges. It does not provide the clear delineated dichotomy between the actual and the virtual. Instead, mimesis is an indexical mediation through which the subject and the object exchange (congenital) affinities. Not unlike the Leonardo surface, the surface of mimesis can be understood as the index of subject-object intermodality, transcendence or participation in the operations of *physis*. Thus, being mimetic provides architecture with a specific and concise view of the architectural envelope as the mediator between the unfolding of nature, subject and self, and the intermodality between subjectivity and the contingencies of its *Umwelt*.

Ecologically speaking, mimesis and empathy do not pertain much to an objective, disinterested *Umgebung*. Such an environment is considered as being simply *out there* to be seized, and meaningless other than for what is there for us to exploit. Neither are they about imitating the ways of natural beings in an attempt to cover up the problems that are symptomatic of our conflict with *physis*. Jakob von Uexküll demonstrates that we cannot communicate with the *Umwelten* of other species. Nonetheless, our *Umwelt* overlaps and is inextricably in tune with those of others.[13] If we disregard this view, functionalist mimesis is nothing but perpetual

9. Hansen, Miriam, "Benjamin, Cinema and Experience: The Blue Flower in the Land of Technology", *New German Critique*, 40, Special Issue on Weimar Film Theory, winter, 1987, pp 179–224, 195.

10. Derrida, Jacques, "White Mythology: Metaphor in the Text of Philosophy", FCT Moore trans, *New Literary History*, 6, 1, On Metaphor, autumn, 1974, pp 5–74, 37. (Emphasis in original).

11. Lakoff, George, and Mark Johnson, *Philosophy in the Flesh: The Embodied Mind and Its Challenges to Western Thought*, New York: Basic Books, 1999, p 268.

12. Lakoff and Johnson, *Philosophy in the Flesh*, p 565.

13. von Uexküll, Jakob, *A Foray into the Worlds of Animals and Humans with a Theory of Meaning*, Joseph D O'Neill trans, Minneapolis: University of Minnesota Press, 2010, Loc. 1417–1451 and 1973–1983. See also: Agamben, Giorgio, *The Open: Man and Animal*, Werner Hamachi ed, Kevin Attell trans, Stanford: Stanford University Press, 2004.

reiteration and versioning of copies of copies. It reinforces further the human-centric, totalising environment that exploits and destroys everything in its path.

The architectural envelope will continue to express the affective intent of the prevailing *dispositifs*. It is not only indexical of the building's form and contents, but also active in the fluctuating relationship between the building and its environment. However, the prevailing notion of a *smart,* responsive, adaptive and/or mimetic architectural envelope appears to promote technology as fetish. It commodifies the natural world, rather than promoting the medi(t)ative qualities between human and natural environments. The approach centred on emulating natural conditions through mechanistic contraptions – the *stuff* that sustains the Junkspace – fails to medi(t)ate and embody the *Umwelt*. The concept of architectural envelope as surface, both abstract and physical, provides that it can act both as an agent of equilibrium and as an apparatus that is in tune with other *Umwelten*.

We can criticise the architectural envelope that displays nothing but the superficial affect-value, fabricating the glamour of the skin without the body, with hypocritical and manipulative motives. We can also criticise the fetishising novelty effects that quickly exhaust the allure. Both tendencies of the architectural envelope only cover up an increasingly excessive, obese and dysfunctional body. The mechanisation of buildings and the architectural envelope fetishise "the desubjectivised multitude of partial objects".[14] As the surface of medi(t)ation between matter and affectation, the architectural envelope should embody the unfolding of various relations and forces between the building and its *Umwelt*. This unfolding provides not only the aesthetic qualities of the building, but also an approach to reconsidering the "disinhibitors" of the human *Umwelt* that have dictated the terms of a human habitat.

14. Žižek, *Organs without Bodies*, p 173.

This vantage point serves the purpose of architectural enclosure as the surface of medi(t)ation and conflation. The surface thus indicates the architectural envelope and the facades that are interwoven, neither arbitrary nor capricious. Ecologically conscious architecture articulates surface as a means of sublating the interior-exterior relationship. It helps weave, pleat and mediate the artificial in relation to the natural. Seen this way, the architectural envelope as surface not only provides the agent of affectation appealing to our senses, but also embodies the quintessential qualities of human space that is empathetic to and mimetic of the natural environment.

Sang Lee teaches architecture at Delft University of Technology. He is a co-founder of Aleatorix, an experimental R&D practice based in Rotterdam and Berlin. He has taught and served as a critic in numerous universities in the US and the EU. Sang edited and published *Aesthetics of Sustainable Architecture* in 2011, and *The Domestic and the Foreign in Architecture* in 2007. He is currently working on *Architecture in the Age of Apparatus-Centric Culture* and *Meta-Architecture: Semiospheres Beyond Algorithm*, both forthcoming in 2016. ➤

SHARED TERRITORY AND SHARED NECESSITY —

Alexander Wright

In writing this piece on agendas in architecture I feel somewhat uneasy, as I have yet to be convinced that architecture requires those in education to articulate any new agenda or ideology. Such agendas largely fail to have the desired impact on architectural practice as it is commonly prosecuted. Conceptual models are often presented in language which appears to have evolved exclusively for the purposes of academic discourse: it is at best ambiguous and at worst impenetrable to anyone who carries out their day-to-day work beyond the environment of academia. However, my personal frustration with the language employed is not the sole reservation I hold with respect to such agenda setting. More significant is its lack of efficacy in influencing the development of higher education, the fate of the profession or the built environment.

The agenda I would like to posit is one for architectural education and the profession rather than for architecture. Although architectural education and the profession enjoy a close relationship, they are characterised by separate concerns as much as shared ones. They occupy two distinct if overlapping territories. The agenda to which I find myself increasingly drawn is concerned with extending and exploiting their shared territory to the benefit of both. Such an agenda results from accommodating their current, pressing needs.

Universities are driven by concerns quite distinct from those of the profession, and they have to respond to conditions specific to the higher education sector rather than those of the construction industry. The two principal areas of academic activity are teaching and research. Consideration of each should be prefaced by my obvious desire to see architectural education thrive in a very competitive environment. Leaving aside the competition between schools of architecture across the world for students, staff, resources and esteem, our shared interest in this context is to see architecture compete effectively with other subjects. Architecture has to compete with other disciplines for the most talented students, and for all the resources which enable it to operate within higher education.

The profession currently finds itself under pressure as a result of the expansion of competing disciplines into its peripheral and core activities. Architects' fee levels have become squeezed to the point where their earnings place them well below occupations that require little or no academic training. In the UK, coal miners and train drivers receive higher average incomes than architects[1] despite UK architects being ranked as the second highest paid in Europe.[2] In order to reverse this long-term decline in relative earnings, the profession needs to demonstrate its value, and its potential to add value, to existing and potential clients. Highly valued professions rely on their expertise, and such expertise is often based on continuous research and development. In short, for a profession to thrive it typically requires a vibrant research culture with an accessible evidence base capable of being used to demonstrate its value. This is something the architectural profession has to date struggled to establish.

1. The UK Office of National Statistics provides data on the median earnings of a wide variety of professions and occupations. In 2010, architects ranked 44th by occupation, with coal miners ranked 28th and train drivers ranked 24th.

2. The Architects Council of Europe published its report *The Architectural Profession in Europe 2012* in December 2012, in which UK architects' average earnings were ranked second in Europe below only Luxembourg, Table 4–1, p 53.

THE RESEARCH AGENDA

Any research-intensive higher education institution seeks to demonstrate a strong research base, as measured by the common currencies of outputs, impact, grant capture and size.

Over the past 50 years, as architecture sought to establish itself within universities, its research focus tended to be aligned with the methodology of existing academic subjects. This created a research base which universities could understand, since it followed established processes and parameters. For many schools, this research was humanities-based, centred on the study of history and theory. This activity over recent decades has produced outstanding scholarship and many individual careers have flourished as a result. As research funding comes under growing pressure in the UK and elsewhere, the balance of available funding is shifting focus onto future areas for development.

Arts funding is increasingly hard to come by, and competition for available grants is fierce. Schools that have developed a research base which includes subject areas within the science and technology spheres have been the first to see that STEM (Science, Technology, Engineering and Mathematics) funding is likely to be a more fertile area in the near and medium-term future. Research in many fields, among them low energy design, low carbon design and innovative materials, is being expanded, as the demand for qualified staff in these fields indicates. Schools which evolved within arts faculties may beg to differ, but the metrics around grant capture would suggest that grant income is flowing more to STEM than to the Arts. If this appears to reduce research to simple economics, then, albeit with laudable exceptions, in general this is representative of the concerns expressed in current planning discussions. In the real world of higher education finance, research follows the money more reliably than the converse.

Whilst humanities and science-based academic research in some proportion or another has provided a core aspect of any school of architecture, the discipline has been singularly unsuccessful in realising the potential of practice-based research. Innovation in practice represents a vast and relatively untapped source of new knowledge in academic terms. The agenda for architectural research over the next decade could be to agree a methodological basis for the execution, assessment and dissemination of such research. The EU's Horizon 2020 framework, in using the phrase "research and innovation", would appear to open the door to work focused as much on innovation as research, and in so doing it appears perfectly aligned with the potential of practice-based research in terms of devising and assessing novel solutions. Its 80 billion euro funding stream is already focusing the attention of just about every institution across Europe.

One agenda for architects and architectural education would therefore appear to coalesce around the area of practice-based research. The forces of mutual attraction resulting from the potential shared benefits of collaboration are only opposed by the pragmatic difficulties of finding a partner, and being entirely unsure about how to consummate the relationship. Devising an agreed etiquette has proved elusive, but the potential prize maintains this area at the top of the agenda.

THE TEACHING AGENDA

Architectural education resides somewhat uncomfortably in many universities. It often seeks to stand outside normal practice and processes as a result of its inherent nature. Other disciplines frequently fail to understand studio culture, the need for dedicated studio space, or the need for vast numbers of external, practising tutors to deliver core parts of its courses. Fortunately, architecture's use of project-led, problem-based learning, which it has employed through the studio method for decades, today appears far-sighted and ahead of its time. As content delivery in the form of the traditional lecture appears increasingly antiquated and inefficient, the studio would seem to provide exactly the sort of flipped learning that the MOOC-based (massive open online courses) future of higher education can embrace, although perhaps less quickly and dramatically than the MOOC evangelists might predict.

Following the UK's withdrawal of all direct state funding for undergraduate architectural education, with the result that students are now burdened by the full cost of their education through debt, an inconvenient truth has become more markedly apparent. Architects rarely earn enough to make embarking on five full years of traditional academic study a rational financial decision. What are needed are more pathways through architectural education to enable individuals to navigate more attractive routes through to the levels of required competence that the profession quite rightly demands. This provides another potentially timely coalescence of interests between architectural education and the profession: the acquisition of graduate attributes, in part through work-based study. The return to pupillage may be a step too far, but the retention of the existing rigid norm of university-based study is only likely to lead to the gradual relative decline of architectural education. In changing and uncertain times, institutions need the freedom to innovate in response. Any species that fails to adapt to a changing climate can rarely look forward to a flourishing future.

CONCLUSION

Architects need to exert influence and possess authority in order to have an impact on our emerging built environment. They would benefit from being able to demonstrate the value they add and the value they create through robust and accessible research. Higher education institutions provide ready collaborators for such research, prompted by their own need to generate new knowledge and innovation through funded research. Architectural education and the profession would benefit from continuing to attract the brightest and best students. In order to do so, the pathways to the profession need to be various, varied and attractive, in competition with those of all other disciplines. Architecture will survive, but without some change in direction it may be that it does so increasingly, and regrettably, with less involvement from architects.

Architecture does not need an agenda, but architectural education, in collaboration with the architectural profession, certainly does.

Professor Alexander Wright is Head of Architecture and Associate Dean at the University of Bath. He is an elected representative on the board of the ARB, Chair of the UK Architectural Education Review Group and Chair of the Standing Conference of Heads of Schools of Architecture.

CELEBRATING ARCHITECTURE — ENJOYING RESEARCH —

Manuel Gausa

1. CELEBRATING ARCHITECTURE

1 The last few decades have confirmed the evidence of a spectacular change of scale in the definition of our spaces of interaction and sociability – of our own habitats – which has to do with the current increase in mobility and long-distance communication, the delocalisation of exchanges, and the capacity for technological and material transformation of our environment.

2 Faced with the progressive *infrastructural* and *informational* (and not just formal or functional) dimension of an evolving territory, defined by layers of information and definition and networks of interchange and flow, our challenge as architects is that of proposing new formulations of space and of architectural design in synergy "in" and "with" a real, virtual and vocationally more complex environment – or, if you prefer, one more open to complexity.

In actual fact, the notion of complexity alludes to this: to the capacity for combining and synchronising, activating and interactivating, multifarious and not always harmonious data and programmes in a single infrastructural framework of (inter)relation.

3 A defensive (or overly cautious) vision of the architectural intervention – the more traditional kind – would seek to work "from" complexity in order to limit and to "essentialise" manifestations of it: to minimise and tranquilise movements by stabilising trajectories, purifying and limiting information, fixing perimeters. By prefiguring, in the name of greater control, its particular "irregular" dynamics.

A more optimistic and purposeful vision of the architectural intervention would propose (to itself) to work "with" complexity in order to mobilise and maximise its evolutive and combinatory potential; working with a new type of operative logic, capable of synthesising the shift from the stable to the dynamic, the additive to the interactive and the unitary to the heterogeneous. From the pure to the definitively impure.

Working from complexity in order to simplify it, or working with complexity in order to celebrate it.

4 Today, we are present at a change of paradigm in architectural thinking. From an architecture based on a static logic we have moved, or are moving, towards an architecture based on a dynamic logic; one that is more impure, irregular and definitively interactive: in interaction with an environment, a context, a society and a creative and scientific culture permanently attentive to the diversity and complexity of a definitively *informational* space-time.

A new type of "alternative" or advanced logic stemming from the actual conditions of our environment and associated with factors of:

— Dynamism (Evolutivity)
— Complexity (Simultaneity)
— Diversity (Plurality)
— Transversality (Connectivity)
— Interaction (Interchange)

Factors that are precisely the ones we now have to explore. Those of a new logic that is more open because it is less fixed, because it is more relational and interactive.

5 A more *open* logic, which is no longer that of classic metaphysical continuity, nor that of postmodern calligraphy (associated with a yearned-for *composition of space*), nor again that of functional modern objectuality, associated with a given *position in space*, but that of contemporary, operative interactivity, associated with a potential *arrangement of spaces*.

If the object of classical composition was the symbolic or metaphysical reproduction of the past, and if the modern position was deemed to be that of the functional production of the new, then the object of the contemporary arrangement is the interactive coproduction of the simultaneous, the real and the virtual, based on a new type of architectural thinking and standpoint that intends to celebrate, articulate and promote the diversity of our time, and to do this, indeed, through interaction.

6 This is the ultimate condition of architectural design: namely to generate and materialise relations, and not just forms, in space.

From an architecture traditionally understood as an "inert object" we ought to move on today to an architecture purposefully conceived as a dynamic, relational environment. An architecture constructed from a mechanism of interaction and resonance with the new sensibility, a sensibility open to the complex, evolutive processes that mark the beginning of this century. Therein lies the innovatory potential of a new concern in terms of design, that of an architecture able to express its own movement, but also the different solicitations that convoke and configure it. An architecture able to resonate and to resound, to work beyond boundaries and traditional dichotomies such as architecture and landscape, city and territory, etc.

7 The contemporary interest in tackling transverse fields involving urbanism, architecture and landscape responds to the interest in moving between boundaries, logics and scales (to recognise and to transgress them), but also to understanding architecture as a relational environment rather than a mere formal or functional object, with all that this implies in terms of constructional and interpretative planning, and (why not?) narrative interaction in and with the environment.

A relational and active volition, then, or reactive volition, if you prefer. That of an architecture which intends to formulate interaction and interchange, plurality and diversity, complexity and mixity, and connection and transversality.

8 Indeed, on the basis of this new logic we have to rethink such traditional issues as the notions of order, form and organisation, and those of architectural structure and expression. And to also rethink our desire as architects not to renounce our first and basic mission, which is to help create a better habitat. That is, a type of habitable environment in consonance with the ambitious anxieties — more than with the contingent demands — of actual society. Not with its tastes, but rather with its ambitions; namely, the ability to foster intellectual curiosity, social projections and cultural expectations in the presence of more imaginative and stimulating types of built settings.

<u>9</u> To develop intersecting settings in which authenticity does not reside in some kind of essentialist basis, but in that open-ended process of interchange and interaction intended to work simultaneously with:

— The context and beyond the context.
— The location and the city. The city and geography.
— Nature and technology.
— Concepts more than ideas.
— Formulation more than figuration.
— Trajectories more than objects.
— Fabrication more than construction.
— Synthetic registers more than analytical layouts.
— Processes more than events.
— Arrangements – and devices – more than "designs".

2. ENJOYING RESEARCH

<u>10</u> At this time of shared exploration, architecture must go back to being, in point of fact, a collective cultural adventure and no longer a mere register of brand names or individual personalities. This adventure involves innovatory lines of research, shared horizons, and narratives that are more stimulating and exciting in their individual and adventurous decodification.

Above and beyond the habitual gloss on "singular trajectories", "iconic personalities", "unique experiments" or "revered teachers", we are interested in an architecture that is able to generate shared processes of investigation: trajectories capable of revealing the evolution of a new architecture that is diverse and enabling because it is connected and promulgated in relation to the conditions of its own time.

<u>11</u> What must be encouraged in the profession, in education, and in research, is generosity rather than rivalry, teamwork, and also inter-teamwork, networking (also without networks), near and far, side by side and at a distance. Working with discipline and indiscipline, between disciplines and beyond the discipline. The combining of rigour and audacity, analysis and intuition, personal affirmation and common concerns, the close at hand and the cosmopolitan.
Intellectual respect and emotional admiration.
Intimate conviction and enthusiastic curiosity.
Without exclusiveness, competitiveness or rivalry.
Without any stupid jealousy or cautious suspicion.
Without any more anxiety about making mistakes or fear of ridicule.
Enjoyment of the emotion of experiencing architecture and proposing architectures.

<u>12</u> Students are no longer former "disciples", but new and virtual *associates* in the combined research and production programme that is called for today. The profession gives way to research, and the transmission of certainties gives way to the construction of criteria: the criteria of intervention.

The idea of a school as a CENTRE (as a centralised formative space) gives way, then, to the idea of a school as a LABORATORY (as a creative and investigative networking environment).

13   Trusting in emergent talent and energy, and combining the rigour and deliberation of experience with youthful imagination and enthusiasm are therefore crucial in guaranteeing the purposeful quality of an authentic educational environment.

A school with a genuine vocation for feedback and leadership cannot let talent go to waste. On the contrary, it must incorporate talent, each generation's talent, as a whole. Not on the basis of mentorship but by promoting it through encouraging the drive towards initiative, and by providing access to areas of projection and responsibility. This is what we try to do in the IAAC in Barcelona or in the ADD in Genoa.

14   A change in the actual university model is to be glimpsed on the horizon. We are witnessing the final defensive death throes of a model overly rooted in totemic and hierarchical structures that are excessively rigid due to academic restrictions. It is obvious that we must open these structures up to society itself, but above all, to the emergence of talent and purposeful energy.

The transverse field of architecture forms part of the academic and scientific community, but also of the cultural, productive and creative community. That is its greatness....

15   Above and beyond economic strategies and productive cost-effectiveness centred on commercial and competitive efficiency, didactic production and scientific research have to be capable of generating *cultural value* – ideological, intellectual, ethical and proactive positioning – and of generating not only knowledge, but also creative energy and stimulus.

To celebrate architecture and to enjoy research: today, this ought to be a potential shared discourse, fundamental to vindicating – and to designing – the transverse role of an old, extremely old, *(trans)discipline*.

Manuel Gausa is an architect and holds a PhD. He is Dean of the IAAC, Institut d'Arquitectura Avançada de Catalunya and Professor and Director of the ADD, Scuola di Dottorato in Architettura e Design, UNIGE-Genoa. He was Director of the magazine *Quaderns d'Arquitectura I Urbanisme*, 1991–2000, and co-founder of the group Actar. ⚊

ARCHITECTURE'S GOLDEN MOMENT (OR: HOW IT WORKS) — A POLEMIC AND A PLEA FOR RESEARCH

Urs Hirschberg

Has there ever been a time when architects didn't complain? About the lack of understanding society has for our profession, about the economic times that do not allow us to build, and about those architects that just do not seem to get it.... I do not mean to belittle any of these problems, they are real and they are annoying (especially the last one....), but at the same time, shouldn't we admit that this state of crisis is rather usual? Architecture is what it is partly because it is in constant crisis. And architects would not be architects if we could not complain about it, come up with new theories about just why the current situation is worse than ever, and imagine a world where everything is better. We love doing it. Sometimes it even seems it is what we do best.

Therefore, personally I do not find the introductory statement of this publication worrying. It diagnoses "a climate of in(st)ability and insecurity in the current architectural discourse, a wide variety of notions of space, a continued fragmentation, a reflex of withdrawal". It states that "Architects are not ready to think the big thoughts anymore, they are on shaky grounds, unsure of their own mission and therefore unable to offer a vision for society".

Indeed: wouldn't we all like to offer a vision to society! And has society not been desperately waiting for us to do so!

Of course times are hard and the world is a complicated place. Life is challenging, but not only for architects. So let me propose a less pessimistic take on the current situation: depending on how you look at it, the present offers a wider and richer set of possibilities and opportunities than our profession has seen in a long time – if ever. This is not a time to lament. This is a time to seize these opportunities, a time to realise that architecture matters and that we can really make a difference if we want to.

Consider the following facts:

— The world population is rising, as is the standard of living worldwide. In the years to come, humanity will be building more than ever before in its history.

— Awareness of the impact of cities and buildings on our many environmental and societal problems is rising, creating an urgent need for our expertise.

— Equally rising (at least in Europe) is an awareness of the value of our cultural heritage, leading to a higher appreciation of thoughtful and context-aware architecture.

So what's the upshot of this? The world cannot wait for our vision, it needs our expertise. Now!

The question is: can we deliver? That is where the actual problem lies. Rather than tackling the real, pertinent problems which our communities and cities are facing these days: the lack of good cheap housing, social segregation, sprawl, the waste of energy and resources, destruction of the landscape, pollution, erosion of civic space – architecture schools have busied themselves with discussions about form or style. Or notions of space. Or the work of star architects. Meanwhile, others are doing the building. In some countries the percentage of buildings that are designed by architects is below five per cent and further decreasing.

Here is one reason why: architecture schools are lagging behind other disciplines because of their attitude to research. Our research tradition is weak, we are slow to innovate, slow to integrate new ideas or new thinking and slow to change. This is reflected in our teaching and therefore ultimately also in our students: architects are losing ground in practice because we do not equip our graduates with the knowledge and skills or the desire to do research. Therefore they lack the skills to tackle the complex problems they are confronted with in practice.

I'm not saying that our graduates are incompetent. The best among them are very good at coming up with beautiful schemes, impressive forms and spaces, or elegant solutions for tricky programmes. These are essential skills at the very core of our profession and they alone are hard to come by. But despite their design competences, architecture graduates are at a loss when it comes to promoting the performative qualities of their work, such as: how does their project influence urban life? How does it help society preserve resources, reduce waste or improve social integration? Our graduates cannot provide satisfactory answers to these questions because our discipline cannot. We know what has been built in the past and what can be built today. We know how a building can fulfil a programme and how it can be made to look good. But today, that is no longer good enough. When it comes to accounting for how our buildings perform, we are out of our depth. We argue with our hopes and our expectations rather than with evidence. Arguing for a new project becomes a question of persuasion and belief, because that is really all we have to go by. In important ways we do not know how architecture works. Why? Perhaps it is true that there are some things about people and buildings that one can never know beforehand. Mostly, however, I think it is because we have not really bothered to try to find out. Which is another way of saying that we have not done anywhere near enough substantial research into these vital and essential matters.

To be clear: it is a good thing that architecture is one of the few remaining generalist disciplines. At architecture schools we do not educate "experts", but creative thinkers who can address many types of problems and cross many types of borders. We are not simply builders or artisans and we should always resist being pigeonholed – whether it be as artists, technicians or theorists. This refusal to become "experts" may in part explain why we have not developed a more impressive research track record. But being generalists is also part of our identity. To deserve its name, research in architecture needs to be as complex and as generalist as our discipline itself. The problem isn't about being generalists. It is about our not being *generalist researchers* as well! Now is the moment to change.

Consider Horizon2020, the new research framework of the EU, which is being rolled out at this time. It has architecture written all over it! Not only because it mentions smart cities and communities, resource efficiency, energy efficiency, building, construction, cultural heritage and societal change, but also because it explicitly values generalist thinking. So we should apply for it, team up and send in our proposals. Of course Horizon2020 is not the only research fund that has realised the societal relevance of these topics, there are many others, international as well as national and local.

Given that our track record is not as good as that of other disciplines, some of our proposals might fail to get funding, at least initially. But we should nevertheless try, and keep trying. Without external funding most architecture schools' budgets are much too constrained to allow for sponsoring in-depth research activities. Therefore architecture schools must put funded research at the top of their agenda. And they must team up with other disciplines and with practice to conduct it. Thereby, slowly but surely, we will develop what we currently lack: a respected tradition of rigorous research. We need relevant research and genuinely architectural research. We need research by design, research through design, research as design. We need research that is discussed and respected by the best in our field. Our best students must become researchers, our best practitioners must be researchers, and links between research and practice must be strengthened. We have a long journey ahead.

Rather than theorising about "border thinking", let us accept that the world does not need a new buzzword or another new vision. It is waiting for the results of our work. Nowadays, that specifically includes our research. There are plenty of real problems for architecture to address. We need to find out much more about how architecture works! The current crisis is a golden moment for architecture! This is our time and our opportunity to finally get serious about architectural research. Let's seize it.

Urs Hirschberg is Professor of Architectural Representation and New Media at Graz University of Technology. He holds an architecture diploma and a doctorate from ETH Zürich. Prior to his appointment in Graz, he served as Research Assistant and Lecturer at ETH Zürich and as Assistant Professor of Design Computing at the Harvard Graduate School of Design. Founding director of the TU Graz Institute of Architecture and Media, Hirschberg served as Dean of the TU Graz architecture faculty for nine years and is a founding editor of *GAM*, the Graz Architecture Magazine. A former president of the European Association of Architectural Education, he is a co-founder of the Architecture Research Network ARENA. He currently directs the interdepartmental research field on sustainable systems at TU Graz.

A UNIFIED AGENDA FOR ARCHITECTURE —
THE BUILT ENVIRONMENT AS FRAME AND INTERFACE OF COMMUNICATION

Patrik Schumacher

My contribution proposes what the editors deny, namely the "re-establishment of a synthetic whole, an epistemological construction in which everything is rationally ordered into a coherent whole". What I am proposing is a global, unified epochal style for architecture, urbanism, and all the design disciplines (parametricism),[1] argued for within a comprehensive, unified theory of architecture/design (the theory of architectural autopoiesis) which is embedded within an overarching theory of society (Luhmann's social systems theory).[2]

Clarity and unity of agenda are necessary preconditions for effective collective action.[3] Such clarity and unity must not be based on prejudice or a simplistic world view. The world within which architecture must try to redefine its role and agenda seems much more complex and uncertain than the world in which architectural Modernism made its mark 60 years ago. Many have come to believe that this world is too fragmented and contested to allow for a unified architectural agenda analogous to the Modern Movement. This scepticism coincides with the general distrust for grand social theories since the crisis of Marxism and other modernisation theories. The 1970s exposed the naivety of those theories' expectations for global industrialisation, democratisation, the expansion of general social welfare and the smoothing of business cycles via democratic steering. The world had become a rather more complex and unpredictable place. This condition was reflected in the new theoretical sophistication of post-structuralist theory. New loops of theoretical reflection — on language, discourse, audience, institutional interests, etc — circumscribed and relativised the substantial claims that might still be made in social and cultural analysis. However, the registration of the new cultural complexities was accompanied by scepticism towards attempts at grand theoretical synthesis. So there is no comprehensive post-structuralist theory of society. Instead, we witness a proliferation of perspectives. At the same time, Modernism in architecture/design gave way to a pluralism of styles.

However, the increased complexity and diversification of social phenomena unfolds more than ever within a single, integrated social world. Thus there exists the greater possibility (and necessity) of a unified theory, one that is much more complex than earlier theories and which includes the new post-structuralist insights and loops of reflection.

There is indeed such a social theory, one that can cope with this new level of complexity and uncertainty. This is Niklas Luhmann's theory of "functionally differentiated society", embedded in his "social systems theory", based on complexity theory and the theory of autopoiesis. My unified theory of architecture is explicitly built on Luhmann's theory and can be read as a new component within his theoretical system.

1. My conceptual definition of parametricism is that all elements of architecture become parametrically malleable and responsive to each other, and to their wider contexts, in the pursuit over an overall increase of interdependencies (density of relations). My operational definition of *parametricism* comprises a set of *formal* a priori principles together with a set of *functional* a priori principles. Negative formal principles (taboos): no inert geometric elements (like cubes, cylinders, spheres), no simple repetition of elements, no collage; ie, no juxtaposition of unrelated elements. Positive formal principles (dogmas): all elements are variable, all systems of elements are differentiated, all elements and all differentiated systems correlate (interdependent). Negative functional principles (taboos): no fixed stereotypes, no social homogenisation, no segregative zoning. Positive functional principles (dogmas): all functions are parametric/variable event scenarios, all programmes are domain differentiated, everything communicates with everything else.

2. My underlying epistemology is radical constructivism, which I understand to be a variant of pragmatism. The theory reflects itself as a designed theoretical construction that sets itself as contingent and understands itself as a provisional attempt to integrate a multiplicity of insights. It evaluates itself in terms of its comprehensiveness, fruitfulness and relevance to contemporary architectural practice.

3. When we speak of collective action today we no longer mean organised or centrally coordinated action. What is implied here is a spontaneous convergence within an open-ended network of communications.

50

The key categories in Luhmann's theoretical edifice are the concept of communication and the concept of social system. Social systems are systems of communication. World society is understood as the totality of all communications. These communications are self-organised (autopoiesis) into systems (networks) primarily according to the principle of functional differentiation (function systems).[4] Accordingly, my theory of architecture theorises the discipline as an evolving system of communications (discourse) that takes universal and exclusive responsibility for innovation in the built environment, in functional differentiation from engineering, science, art, politics, law, economics and so forth. The specific responsibility of architecture/design concerns the social/communicative functionality (as distinct from the technical/engineering functionality) of the built environment. Spaces are theorised as framing communications that function as invitations and premises for all the interactions that take place within them. Each territory/frame is embedded within a system of frames, which can be understood as a system of signification.

Society can only evolve with the simultaneous ordering of space. The life process of society is a communication process that is structured by an ever more complex and richly diversified matrix of institutions and communicative situations. The built environment orders and stabilises this matrix of institutions and makes it legible. Innovation in the built environment participates in the expansion, differentiation and integration of this network of communicative situations. Contemporary network society demands that we continuously browse and scan as much of the social world as possible in order to remain connected and informed at all times. Our ambition as architects and urban designers must be to spatially elaborate more simultaneous choices of communicative situations in dense, perceptually palpable and legible arrangements. The visual field must be rich in interactional opportunities and information about what lies behind the immediate field of vision.

My thesis is that the built environment should be conceived and designed as a three-dimensional, 360 degree, layered interface of communication. The more it becomes simultaneously visible, the more it can communicate. But that is not enough. Its communicative capacity depends on the coherency of its internal order, so that what is visible allows for inferences about what is invisible or not yet visible. This depends on the consistency of its form-function correlations, so that a positional or morphological distinction or difference makes a predictable difference in terms of an expected social interaction pattern or social function. Thus the built environment's communicative capacity is enhanced the more the architectural order and morphology employed is designed as a coherent system of signification.

To this end I am calling for the refoundation of architectural semiology. Architectural semiology can now be effectively operationalised within a pertinent design methodology under the auspices of parametricism: parametric semiology. The patterns of communicative interaction can be modelled via programmed agents that respond to the encoded environmental clues. This implies that the meaning of architecture can enter the digital model and thus becomes the object of cumulative design elaboration. The system of signification works if the agents consistently respond to the relevant positional and morphological clues, so that anticipated behaviours can be read from the articulated environmental configuration. As agents cross significant thresholds, their behavioural rules are modulated. Territorial distinctions thus order and coordinate interaction patterns. Space defines the situation and solicits the appropriate individual agent's behaviours. The framing architectural communication informs the participants' expectations. Their behavioural dispositions are harmonised so that a specific cooperative event scenario can emerge.

The meaning of architecture and the prospective life processes it frames and sustains are becoming a direct object of creative speculation. This new

51

capacity to operationalise architectural semiology is compatible with architecture's enhanced understanding and handling of its programme, as promoted in the functional heuristics of parametricism: the function or programme of architecture is no longer conceived as a set of separate stereotypes (schedule of accommodation) that can be handled by labelling plan diagrams. Rather, the programme is conceived in terms of dynamic, parametrically variable event scenarios that unfold and evolve across time and space. This way of handling and modelling programmes via crowds of (environmentally informed) agents also allows for the consideration of multiple audiences with different purposes and roles. The meaning of spaces can thus be made relative to audiences. Furthermore, typical, anticipated interaction patterns (institutions or communicative situations) are emergent rather than imposed phenomena that result from rule-based interaction. This increases architecture's capacity to speculate about and simulate its role and agency with respect to sociologically innovative forms of interaction, and avoid an ever more untenable reduction to stereotypes. To summarise: my agenda for architecture is to push parametricism into the mainstream by making its advantages compelling within our communication-intensive network society, through the refoundation of architectural semiology as agent-based parametric semiology.

Patrik Schumacher is partner at Zaha Hadid Architects and has since 1988 been the co-author of most key projects. He studied philosophy, mathematics and architecture in Bonn, London and Stuttgart and completed his PhD at the Institute for Cultural Science, Klagenfurt University. In 1996, he founded the Design Research Laboratory at the Architectural Association in London. In 2010/2012 he published his two-volume theoretical opus magnum *The Autopoiesis of Architecture*. His architectural writings are available on www.patrikschumacher.com. ▼

ARCHITECTURE'S CONTINUING CONTRIBUTION –

Christopher Platt

Architecture must save the world! The planet is doomed!

I sometimes hear this when in discussion about the issues that contemporary architecture needs to address. For some colleagues, architecture above all else must atone for the environmental sins of the past. Their argument is as powerful as it is clear; namely that there is no greater issue to address than climate change. It is difficult to disagree with this position. However, I sense a similarity between this stance and the preoccupation in the 1960s with sociology, and in the 1970s and 1980s with semiology. I feel this is yet another fig leaf that helps some people avoid the cultural and constructional complexities of the creative design process, and reduces the task of architecture to one single issue. If only our world was that simple.

Architecture is informed by the need to be responsive to changing external influences. Those influences have always varied throughout history, but recently they seem to be changing with increasing acceleration. Contrasting political or religious client authorities; the availability of labour, skills and raw materials; the devastation caused by natural and man-made events; the changing international climate; industrialisation and the globalisation of communications and business; scientific, technological or artistic discoveries; the changing roles within the construction industry; the growth of the public's appetite for design and the tensions between need and want; the exponential rise of environmental standards, the importance of minority rights and a fully accessible built environment. Environmental longevity and programmatic agility are both crucial components for the future of any architecture, but these should be mainstream issues by now, matters to be addressed as a matter of course.

The invitation to write this paper comes with the implicit question about the issues that will shape the built environment of the twenty-first century, issues which our graduates will spend their professional lives addressing. I feel uncomfortable, however, in writing about the next "big thing". There is a strong temptation to accept the presumption that the demands of our time can be identified and articulated in one clearly defined problem for architecture to address, as if the task was no more complex than identifying and then solving a particular mathematical equation. Is it really as simple as identifying that equation and investing our best resources to focus on it? The current climate within architectural practice and education would sometimes have us believe so.

At no other time has our knowledge of the world seemed greater and that same world seemed tinier than it does now. This is in no small way due to our real-time global communication abilities. This situation has not only brought the diversity of our world cascading into a virtual melting pot a click away, but also exported our own private everyday life to anyone we choose to send it to (and some we don't!). We can FaceTime our children back home while simultaneously flying above the Indian Ocean, as a friend of mine did recently on his way to Australia. We are, it seems, at one of those rare moments in history when our social patterns (in this case, being internationally active) and the supportive technology are developing at just the right time to be useful.

For 20-something graduates, a global awareness and ethical perspective has been developing steadily throughout their childhood, particularly at school (in many ways we live in an informed and enlightened culture). Consequently, more of the world has become tangible to them. Whilst that in itself may have no influence at all on how they, as future architects, might, say, detail a facade element or deal with a building contractor, it will certainly have an effect on their 'gathering place' of ideas, which informs the cultural hinterland and value system which they carry with them.

According to Minja Yang "[...] By 2025, the UN projects that nearly two-thirds of the world's population will be living in cities".[1] The twenty-first century is already one of increasing oscillation between proximity and distance, local and global, tradition and innovation, and this looks set to continue. Architecture has been used for many purposes throughout history. As well as to shelter, defend, and to impress, it is employed (and sometimes press-ganged) into making political and cultural statements, to sell ideas, and to advertise brands, movements and values. At times, many of these roles have been adopted simultaneously.

Whether we consider the challenges of the Global North or the Global South, it is tempting to identify architecture's contemporary responsibilities as being focused wholly on humanitarian issues, be it rapid urbanisation or the generation of clean water, sanitation, fresh air and shelter. However, within this international vortex of competing demands, the ability to make the physical world meaningful where the public comes face to face with it, and in ways that go beyond shelter and defence, remains contemporary architecture's most important role. As the world becomes smaller in both our imagination and our experience, so must the importance of creating particularity in places increase. Minja Yang adds, "Defacing a city – places charged with spiritual, emotional and symbolic values – is tantamount to violating part of our identity."[2] The creation of identity, both individually and communally, has been, and perhaps remains, the most significant expression of any architectural act. This will increasingly become a key issue for societies everywhere as the twenty-first century gathers momentum and we continue our engagement in more than one country throughout our lives. As we in the Global North become exponentially logged into the world and the magnitude of its issues, we will be increasingly confronted with the question, within our progressively more global community, of who we are. Our neighbour is no longer someone in the same street, town or country, she is at the other end of the world. Architecture must help us navigate and orientate ourselves through this by providing a stable and meaningful sense of place in order to face life's everyday challenges, as well as operating as the lens through which our understanding may grow.

More and more frequently, we are dwelling in one part of the world whilst designing and building in another, and often for short periods. There are fewer opportunities to fully understand a place and all the nuances and eccentricities of its culture. The responsibility to leave a relevant and meaningful physical mark is enormous. The shadows our buildings cast onto those parts of the planet must be benevolent ones. A country's identity is experienced and understood to a large extent through its built environment, and this will increasingly be the case as urbanisation accelerates across the planet. We are all aware of how fragile a country's identity is and how swiftly it can be eroded by contemporary development advocating "progress" and "relevance", particularly in a globally competitive climate. China,

1. Yang, Minja, "Unesco Cultural Conventions for Sustainable Urban Development", *Context: Built, Living and Natural*, vol 1, spring/summer, 2008, pp 6–15.

2. Yang, "Unesco Cultural Conventions for Sustainable Urban Development", pp 6–15.

for example, is in its infancy in the domain of conservation/preservation and has struggled recently with the tensions between heritage and "progress". Within this context, it is tempting to see architecture as some kind of international, cultural NGO. This, however, is not architecture's main role. There are times when we must be able to articulate what issues architecture can address, but we must also be aware of its limitations. By creating identity in the physical world, architecture helps us find identity in our private world.

Who, then, is this person best placed to give form to the built environment? History suggests it is those who are both technically competent but also have the ability to "articulate built stuff so that it bears the imprint of human life and feeling".[3] In other words, those whose skill range crosses what can be loosely described as the scientific as well as the artistic spectrum. A particular combination of skills and ways of thinking is now needed to orchestrate the ever-larger group of professionals involved in shaping the built environment. Someone must set the architectural destination, as well as the map and compass in order to get there. Those able to do this are worthy of the title "architect" and are urgently needed. Our architectural schools have a huge role to play in this. Those skills must reach deeper into familiar, traditional areas, but also extend into hitherto unchartered territories, such as collaborative design methodologies learnt from other creative practices; developing and using research in the design process; establishing new ways to remain involved in the entire realisation process, and honing the entrepreneurial and political skills to initiate projects. And there will be more.

The degree to which architecture responds effectively to all these factors grants our historians a lens through which to understand the wider values and ideas about a particular society or community. That dual ability to be both immediately useful for a particular purpose in a particular place, while also being able to reveal knowledge about wider cultural or societal issues, is architecture's continued contribution to the world and our understanding of it. We should be less concerned with what the architecture (and the architect) of the future should look like, and be more preoccupied with ensuring that a suitably responsive environment exists for this to happen.

Christopher Platt is co-founding director of studioKAP architects and Head and Professor of Architecture at the Mackintosh School of Architecture, the Glasgow School of Art.

————————

3. Maguire, R, speech at RIBA Hull Conference, *The Architect's Journal*, 18 August 1976, p 292.

ARCHITECTURE AS A THOUGHT-IMAGE —

Gerard van Zeijl

English interpreter, Laura Vroomen

Architecture can be seen as a collection of thought-images, images for thinking and thoughts for imagining. It is an age-old and lasting union between art and science, between designing and making. This historical and theoretical accumulation has found expression in treatises, architectural drawings and buildings, with the architectural drawing bridging text and image, albeit tentatively. Taken together, these things form the memory of architecture, which Plato called *épistèmè,* and which more recently has been labelled "discourse" and lends itself to an epistemological argument. This in turn forms an unruly, only partly coherent collection, described by Foucault as a collection of fragments: the "archaeology of knowledge".

Within its own field, architecture has autonomous power, but within a more general, social context, it has both a vulnerable and a critical dimension. This is the paradoxical nature of a discipline that straddles both the material and the immaterial world. Architecture is expected to serve and to realise its thought-images through technical means. It can draw on its scientific powers to meet certain standards; but conversely, science cannot do without critical reflection and must be backed up by philosophy, so that its arguments can both prove a point and persuade. Architecture also has a position within the tradition of art, bringing the expression of both power and powerlessness within its reach. Once upon a time the motto "*ars sine scientia nihil est*" – without knowledge, skill is nothing – applied, but where science crosses the moral boundaries of building, art will invoke its irrational yet critical powers.

Art cannot pass ethical criticism if it is guilty of excessive aestheticism, but it can use its powers of analysis where science and philosophy fall short. In posing questions that are beyond our understanding, architecture appeals – without moralising – to the mind or to a mental attitude, the "*theorein*".

While for centuries architecture gave expression to spiritual aspirations, as it did in the temple and the cathedral, the grave and the monument, in recent times it has served a more practical purpose. In either case it seeks to generate freedom by escaping matter. If freedom entails autonomy, such freedom cannot be absolute if architecture wants to express certain values. Against the backdrop of Walter Benjamin's statement on the role of the author, architecture can adopt a stance: that of "relative autonomy". It is architecture's paradoxical condition which burdens it with a huge responsibility, while at the same time imbuing it with a touch of idiosyncrasy. Perhaps architecture is heedful of Kundera's notion as it represents "the unbearable lightness of being".

This brings us to the true driving force behind architecture: the accommodation of human life. During the French Revolution, Jean-Nicolas-Louis Durand argued that "if not for architecture, mankind would have been wiped out". In a sense this echoes Descartes' "*cogito ergo sum*", "I think, therefore I am": "There is architecture, ergo there is life." Needless to say, this argument must be seen in a historical context, especially since his polemic was aimed at the architecture which, with its excessive art and ingeniousness, had deprived mankind of the right to live. His plea for "*une grande utilité*" turns this right into a necessity, and together with Viollet Le Duc laid the foundation for Functionalism, which ultimately foundered on bureaucracy and insularity. By subjecting the design to a method, Durand pioneered the systematisation of architecture and simultaneously introduced the distinction between the engineer and the architect. The engineer would be responsible for public buildings, the architect for housing. But he has a noticeably "vague notion" of the city, calling merely for a reinstatement of the public space, the "*res publica*".

Echoes of Durand's argument can be heard in Le Corbusier's *Vers une architecture*. He used a CIAM congress as a platform to not just argue for an evocative synthesis between the engineer and the architect, but for an *Existenz* maximum rather than minimum, "*une grande utilité*".

Le Corbusier's urban design vision was an integral part of the architectural composition and – just as the Piazza San Marco represented a radical intervention in the Venetian urban fabric – with La Ville Radieuse he advanced an exclusive fabric, a "*tabula rasa*". It would take an entire generation before the existing city would once again form the starting point for architects. Following the typological and morphological research of Marcel Poëte in Paris and Muratori in Venice, Aldo Rossi characterised the city as a civil construction, more specifically a "social work of art". Above all, his famous drawing of the "analogous city" showed a collection of thought-images, centring on the notion of the "monument", which denotes longevity or "permanence". Architects such as Secchi interpret the architectural intervention as "tinkering with a running engine", while Libeskind sees it as reusing parchment, with the "infinite text" of architecture being over-written time and time again, a "palimpsest".

When Panerai, Castex and Depaule criticised these approaches as idealising because of their narrative character, they did so on the basis of the normativity of a "measurable type", an "established" type, which was seen as the building block of the urban tissue and excluded both heroic and literary motifs. By doing so they laid the foundation for an empirical and subsequently pragmatic approach in which architecture and urban planning were looked at within a process of transformation. And so the problematic division between architecture and urban planning could be refuted in favour of an integrated approach.

That said, from the early Middle Ages to the present day, this approach to design has been based on utopian and/or emancipatory thinking, rooted in both a Judeo-Christian model of civilisation and in Marxist ideology, which is similar in many ways. It was, in short, a purposeful architecture, an "intentional" thinking. In the Europe of the 1970s an offensive gathered momentum, which sought to prevent the breakdown of original values. A tsunami of architectural drawings and manifestos was the response to a great anxiety among exasperated residents caused by what Aldo van Eyck described as "flimsy architecture and urban design".

Against the backdrop of much vocal protest by historians such as Manfredo Tafuri, the search was on for a common denominator such as urban renewal. However, despite the often meaningful revival, the resulting debate degenerated into a largely superficial and nostalgic interpretation of architectural history, a radical Postmodernism that resulted in a fanatical reinstatement of form and symbol under the motto "everything goes". At the risk of creating an artificial antithesis between Europe and America, from 1970 the position of The New York Five inspired the belief that architecture would have to liberate itself not only from the anthropocentrism it had subscribed to since Humanism but also from its ideological connotations. Eisenman invoked architecture's textual dimension, arguing that the cleansing of intentional meanings like those of Le Corbusier and

Terragni would free architecture from its "representative" character so it could reveal its "presence". "Architecture without shadow", referring only to itself, as Bekaert put it. And so the question of autonomy reared its head again, as it did in the Netherlands where Weeber made a similar case for a "formal objectivity".

At the same time, Rem Koolhaas exposed the roots of New York's normativity through an ironic form of narrativity. He unmasked the metropolis as a paradoxical mix of European and American motifs and interests, and also indirectly commented on the conventions of the European debate. Within the postmodern debate he was able to float the theory that "architecture should not get in the way". While Aldo Rossi used his architectural drawing "*l'architecture assassinée*" to champion the survival of the urban structure as intentional and as a "collective memory", Koolhaas unleashed his vision of the "generic city", which gave rise – beyond "established" notions in the vein of Panerai *et al* – to architecture as "automonument", an architecture "without qualities", as Robert Musil might have put it. Yet Koolhaas' interventions would not remain neutral. He interpreted this radical energy within the metropolis to shake up a social system.

Both Koolhaas and Tschumi entered the Parc de la Villette competition, but it was the latter who won. Interestingly, neither really operated within a metropolitan fabric, but put an intrinsic quality of architecture to the test. Tschumi did so using a text by Derrida, "*Point de folie – maintenant l'architecture*", and an architectural drawing. As touched on above, here, too, a thought-image bridged the gap between science and art, and between criticism and everyday reality. The follies in Tschumi's design represent a critique of a dominant functionalist thinking by pitting usefulness and sheer fun against one another.

If we take the famous fresco of the philosophical dispute in Raphael's *School of Athens* in the Stanze di Raffaello in Rome – in which Plato and Aristotle form the complementary centre of image and word, of irrationality and rationality and of autonomy and involvement – and continue the line of this dispute to today's discourse, we end up with the two aforementioned architects since they occupy a similar position: Tschumi and Koolhaas.

Tschumi's statement "To really appreciate architecture, you may even need to commit a murder" can be seen as the sublime surrender to architecture as an autonomous principle and, in a way, also as a negation of the world and affirmation of paradise. Koolhaas' plea "towards a non-utopian pragmatism" can be seen as a radical acceptance of the world, albeit in a way described by Adorno as a "negative affirmation" of the consumer's paradise.

Gerard van Zeijl is Emeritus Professor of Theory and History of Architecture at the Department of the Built Environment, Eindhoven University of Technology, the Netherlands. He finished his dissertation on "The Treatises of JNL Durand" in 1990, followed by his research into "The Longlasting Strategies of Architecture and Urbanism", which became a framework for a number of dissertations called "The ABC of Density". ✗

DOUBLING THE AGENDA —
ARCHITECTURAL EDUCATION AS RESEARCH AND PRACTICE

Alejandro Zaera-Polo

Edited version, in collaboration with Loed Stolte

The following text is a revised compilation of fragments taken from an earlier essay by Alejandro Zaera-Polo and an interview he gave. The essay "Methodological Proposal for the Staedelschule Frankfurt", 2001, was published in The Sniper's Log: Architectural Chronicles from Generation-X *(Alejandro Zaera-Polo, Actar 2013); the interview "Equipping the Architect: The Berlage Menu", 2006, was originally published in "Projecting the City: Beyond Mapping", a special issue of* Hunch, 2006.

TRADITIONAL MODELS FOR ARCHITECTURAL EDUCATION

Until now, the development of institutionalised architectural education has been traditionally dominated by two models; namely, the polytechnic model that predominates in Continental Europe and Asia, and the liberal arts model that characterises Anglo-American schools.

The polytechnic model is efficient in maintaining a close relationship between the educational and practice modes of the discipline of architecture since it provides students with a solid technical background for operating in a particular domain of practice. However, it sometimes fails to produce an adequate environment for a research-driven educational model, which is necessary in order to broaden the field of technical possibilities beyond conventional modes, a crucial consideration when training people to operate in increasingly unstable conditions. As a model of education based on the uncritical development of skills and techniques and devoid of a specific project or objective, it tends towards institutional sclerosis and is often unable to offer alternatives within architectural practice.

The liberal arts model has been the fastest growing model of architectural education during the past ten years as a result of the increasing instability of disciplinary models that demand a more research-oriented educational system. The liberal arts model is more efficient in providing students with the necessary critical background to question, search for and select the appropriate skills to approach a specific architectural problem. It also produces students that are more capable of independent thinking and research. However, this model has evolved into a path of internalisation, where the success of the projects relies purely upon their critical capacity and eccentricity, rendering it unable to operate effectively in the practice of the discipline and outside academia in general. As the discipline-based content of this model diminishes in favour of the critical and ideological content of the education, the academic work focuses more on the ideological or stylistic contents instead of developing operative techniques for architectural production. It often leads to schizophrenia between theory and practice and deprives academic experimentation from any real transformative effect on the practice of architecture.

A FOCUS ON THE PRODUCTIVE

The paradigm of the "critical" is part of the intellectual model that became operative in the early twentieth century, based on the notion that in order to be successful and creative we should take a "negative" view toward reality. But the critical, individualist practice that characterised intellectual correctness for most of the twentieth century is no longer adequate in dealing with a culture determined by transformation on a scale and complexity that is difficult to understand. I have talked in the past about a new "productive" rather than "critical" paradigm where the critical is not deployed on whole systems – let's say capitalism versus Marxism, or democracy versus fundamentalism – but at a much more concrete and haptic level. You have to be fundamentally engaged in the processes and learn to manipulate them from the inside. You never get that far into the process as a critical individual. If we talk in terms of the construction of subjectivity, the "critical" belongs to Freud and Lacan, and what I call the "productive", to Deleuze.

A FOCUS ON THE DISCIPLINE

The opportunity to develop alternative models of architectural education relies precisely on the possibility of re-establishing a strong relationship with the world outside the school in order to construct an academic environment capable of once again generating real transformative possibilities for architecture. Rather than focusing postgraduate studies on theorising other disciplines and trying to make a translation into architecture, a programme that inquires into the production of architecture and the problematisation of its techniques would offer an alternative to the current diffusion into cultural studies. While the connection to humanities is positive and interesting, architecture cannot abandon its material, infrastructural nature without entirely losing its agency. Rather than looking for architecture as a translation of other disciplines, a concentration on architectural materials and techniques would explore how to look at everything from an architectural perspective, and how to search for architectural instruments in other disciplines.

The most interesting questions for architectural theory are those of operativity and technology, concerning how new technologies may become the generators of alternative forms of practice. After a period in which discourse about language, style and ideology has dominated the architectural debate, a return to materials and technologies as the natural locus of architectural research appears promising. A "school" used to be given coherence by the use of a certain language or a certain ideological position. Today, it seems perhaps more adequate to find consistency in the instruments used in architectural production. To research the instrumental will make the discipline grow toward integration with emergent economic, cultural and social structures, as opposed to retreating to the suspect ground of an autonomous, historically constructed discipline.

A DOMAIN OF OPERATION

Every successful school of architecture is characterised not only by a consistent series of procedures, languages and approaches, but also by a strong relationship to a domain of real practice. This field or place of external reference becomes the framework of operation, the object of research and the testing ground for this experimentation: for example, London in the 1970s, Barcelona and Los Angeles in the 1980s, or Rotterdam and Zürich in the 1990s. If the work of the school does not have an effect in real practice, the school remains an academic institution with no real capacity to transform reality. A real school needs a project that is operative beyond the academic domain. Otherwise it produces only further

64

schizophrenic dysfunction between theory and practice, limiting the possibility to test the work of the school as an effective device for transforming reality.

A LABORATORY OF ARCHITECTURE

A focus on the development and problematisation of architectural operativity will not be sufficient without the constitution of a true laboratory where every member will have to develop independent research within a common framework. The difference between this model and a master class is that the consistency that establishes the framework is based on an area of research and an objective, not on the reproduction of a master's style or procedure. In contrast to a traditional polytechnic school, where technique is explored without a specific purpose other than developing skills, and in contrast to a traditional liberal arts school, where critique and individual positions are explored devoid of operational content beyond the academic domain, a laboratory has, primarily, a specific operative purpose. A laboratory is not constituted by a closed series of techniques or an infinitely open series of possible individual positions, but by an infinitely open field of technical and theoretical positions with a specific purpose. The objective of a laboratory is to produce a solution to a problem; any technique or position is legitimate as long as it serves to achieve the purpose that is targeted. The discovery of a vaccine for a certain illness, a new theory in physics to explain a particular phenomenon, or the manipulation of certain types of rhythms to produce musical effects are purposes similar to the development of an architectural prototype for an emergent urban condition. In a laboratory, any strategy is adequate for reaching the objective; there are no limits to the approaches and techniques that may be used to solve the problem, and the participants' creativity lies precisely in their originality in defining their approach to the problem.

DOUBLE AGENDA

The education of architects should be aimed at both the development of a consistent, but constantly evolving body of architectural knowledge and skill, and the education of independent individuals who have the capacity to become operative agents beyond the academic realm. This approach disarms the polarisation between the collective and engaged polytechnic education and the individual and detached approach of the liberal arts model. There is no reason to think that engagement with the reality of architectural practice and the development of individual and independent thinking are mutually exclusive. In fact, they complement each other. As educators, we should aim at producing a vital continuum between an elastic yet consistent school framework (architectural laboratory), a constantly evolving realm of practice, and the development of individual and operative research.

As with pilots, football players and musicians, to be a virtuoso, to produce the magic, you need to know the technique so well that you do not need to think about it anymore.

Alejandro Zaera-Polo is the principal of AZPML and a Professor of Architecture at Princeton University, USA.

———

'A REGISTER OF WORDING' — 'DEFENESTRATION' —

Martine De Maeseneer

I chose two titles because of their mutual sound colour. The first aims more at philosophy and the second rather at architecture. That is what I want to discuss: one part is about language, the other part is about form.

With "A Register]court[of Wording" (but I have dropped the "court"), I want to express Henri Bergson's critique addressing philosophy and – by extension – language. Bergson was a fierce defender of forms and flows *tout court*. But what makes such a citation interesting is that when a native Dutch speaker like me reads the English translation of *Creative Evolution* the term "wording" is comprehensible yet easily confused with the Dutch word "becoming". Ironically enough, "wording" in the sense of "becoming" appears to be the epitome of what Bergson is after in his standard work on "streams of thoughts". The point I want to make firstly is that it is these uncontrollable, subconscious, complementary intentions that attract me.

DEFENESTRATION

"Defenestration" is a layered word and immediately attractive because it has something to do with architecture. The word literally means "to throw someone out of a window". By retracing the biblical origin of the word, Jezebel (or Isabel) enters the picture as the story goes back to the Book of Kings at the time of King Solomon.

Focus already on these two words: "Phoenician" and "defenestration". Both are intrinsically related phonetically (in Dutch it even works better). The story goes as follows: in order to obtain access to the Mediterranean Sea, King Ahab of Israel married the Phoenician princess Jezebel. Yet, because Jezebel brought in too much worldly and foreign influence and forced the Phoenician idol Ba'al upon her spouse, the religious leaders had her thrown from the window of the palace after Ahab's death. Since then, Jezebel represents the cosmopolitan, secular life, as opposed to the rural and religious life, as well as the threat that this entails, which is ended by her symbolic fall.

In a Christian context, the words really take on meaning when the defenestration of Jezebel is considered in relation to the crucifixion as a necessary step for the ascension of Jesus.[1] In Jezebel's case, defenestration is not directly related to resurrection. Arguably, there is a phenomenological side where "Jezebel", in the Hebrew meaning of "the dark princess", becomes the patroness of "coloured" women, prostitutes, and by extension, of feminism. There is also a linguistic component. As a proto-alphabet, Phoenician was absorbed almost unchanged into ancient Greek. There are lines that link Jezebel to the founding of the city of Carthage, and later to Alexandria, etc. To paraphrase Walter Benjamin's "A city is a woman is a book" – this therefore relates to Jezebel as well.

So when I put forward a notion such as 'a register of wording' it becomes especially interesting when I can include 'defenestration' as a kind of

1 . Ingraham, Catherine, "Errand, Detour, and the Wilderness Urbanism of John Hejduk", *Forum International*, no 18, May–August 1993, p 85.

underside or subtitle. Let it mature and develop. Within this expanded field of words and letters, I keep searching for 'an' architecture.

THE OBLIQUE

Personally and incidentally, I ran into the "oblique" in association with the word "opaque", another word with a tail (queue). This happened with Colin Rowe's analysis of Le Corbusier's La Tourette monastery: *When approaching the monastery, that blind wall, that psychological dam catches the eye. Yet again it is that diagonal cut of the belfry that pulls a trick. (It is the frame on top after which the building is named): it turns the full face into a profile. You find yourself walking up to the side of a building while around the corner awaits the whole display.*

What attracted me in particular at the time (1987) was a literary passage about Don Quixote (aka "*L'homme qui chute*") appropriating the word "foreshortening", by means of which Colin Rowe wanted to express his encounter with La Tourette. Foreshortening means "to portray or see as shortened or reduced in depth or distance", and relates to Don Quixote's fate of wandering on his Spanish plateau without much perspective. In retrospect, a blind wall with a suspended bell-frame and all the speculation about an unseizable depth behind – how much closer can one get to defining de-fenestration?

During my studies in London, it was made clear to me that space does not just unfold as a direct visual experience, but also *in abstracto*: in the apprehension of the relative depth of things. This involves passing through different spaces, the surpassing of psychological barriers and a change of direction while moving. Space wagers here upon the labyrinthine. These are things that have accompanied me in every design I make.

Phonetically, a word like "foreshortening" clings automatically to the word "hindsight" (which means "wisdom after the event"). It is as if both words denounce "foresight" – doubly rejecting the word.[2] Down with it goes centuries of fascination that regarded intuition or seeing as a form of acquiring knowledge. The tricky thing is that intuition cannot exist without the unimaginable (God, soul, universe), but also not without non-things, for instance "a circle with four corners". Kant pinpointed these as antinomies in what, furthermore, is called the nominal world.[3]

My own fascination with architecture begins with the linguistic prepositions *in*, *for*, *on*, *to*, and *behind*, which articulate a descent from pure geometry over projective geometry to topology. I relate the onset of architecture to play, to piling up blocks, and, for the better or worse, to pushing around chairs, benches and tables.

FROM A REGISTER OF WORDING TO DERRIDA'S MYSTIC WRITING-PAD

A mystic writing-pad is a toy made from a waxed board with a thin sheet of clear plastic on top. It is a simple machine that allows children to sketch or write, lift the plastic to remove the marks, then start drawing or writing anew. Can we also see this as an act of defenestration?

Subsequently, one has to take into account the psychology that Derrida was attracted to. The former imprints that were made stay behind somewhere in the wax, as a result of which one can start philosophising about lost impressions, the 'Thing' left behind. Derrida's argument is that everything begins in a complexion. Manual.

I also consider my own sketchbooks as mystic writing pads.... In my case the amount of pages and the time frame have to be accounted for. Every new design begins with a ritual of binding 200 pages together. For a period of three

2. Sartre, Jean-Paul, "Foresight", *Being and Nothingness*, London: Routledge, 1956, p 125.

3. Störing, HJ, *Geschiedenis van de Filosofie*, Utrecht, 1985, p 21.

weeks I will stay in 'drawing mode' – making shortcuts between the hand and the eye, or is it the hand that tries to outsmart the brain very much in a manner that Don Quixote talks to his arm? The turning of the pages, going down memory lane, implies a kind of forgetting. It is different from the situation where a plan is drawn upon a plan – which nowadays happens by using a computer programme, but in the past meant copying by means of tracing paper.

At stake is the desire to capture the idea immediately, by way of diagrams, thumbnail sketches and with an occasional proto-model in cardboard made on the side. The point is to get there in successive moves before measuring tools (rod, compass, CAD) take over, and not to worry too much about whether the project will fit the available space. This process constitutes the nerve that will eventually show in real afterwards. At first, designing will happen rather routinely in a manner of working from or discarding existing schemes. Often these are traces or trajectories that became compromised or complicated in the past due to competition juries' critiques, or due to problems of 'realisation'. Soon, though, one will reach a point where the proverbial 'scales fall from the eyes' and one comes across an improbable match. A de-click.

One might call this a tentative search for something new; a process that oscillates between the precision of a clock and the undetermined mistiness of a cloud. Some three weeks and 200 pages later, however, I am always struck by finding the preliminary design complete.

NON-LINEARITY

What has architecture in common with literature, except a similar ending? A certain tension has built up over the ages between philosophy on the one hand and metaphysics on the other, and between language and form. A word such as deconstruction fits into 'the detente of that arch'. Put differently and closer in time, the twentieth century was marked by metaphysics in flux and an outpouring of philosophy. Literature tried to slip along in these temporisations, with its pre- and re-tentions, using architecture as a conductor, lightning rod or punch ball. Dualism.... It is that arch that had to come down....

In his *Tractatus*, Wittgenstein subjected language to an intensive logical reasoning process, only to arrive at the disappointing conclusion that "language cannot step out of itself" and that language is too limited in its ability to explain things. As such, Wittgenstein declared "hermeneutics prove to be hermetic". Deconstruction in the sense of "retracings" means that, in the first place, we have to move away from a language of substantives and substances alike. We have to start juggling with adjectives, colours, pre-positions.

MDMA (Martine De Maeseneer Architects) has been around for 25 years of practicing, theorising and teaching within an international forum of schools, colloquia and competitions. In 2011 their project the Bronks Theatre Brussels was awarded as the first-ever Belgian finalist in the European Mies van der Rohe Award for Architecture. Two books appeared in conjunction with individual exhibitions: The In$_{di}$visible Space, Antwerp, 1993; and Ideality-3-Lost, Brussels, 1997. Essays published (with such titles as "Aperitif Time", "What Matters" and "Parsing Traps") have been adding up as chapters in a more substantial yet unpublished book. From 2001 to 2003, De Maeseneer was a unit master at the AA in London, currently she is teaching at KULeuven Faculty of Architecture, campus LUCA, Brussels/Ghent. Within the MDMA practice, there is a continuous search for an expanded field of patterns, motives, logos, plots, timbres – trying to give architecture a countenance that draws upon 'writing'. Ironically so, the choice made from the onset to theorise in a tradition of Venturi-Scott Brown, Aldo Rossi and Rem Koolhaas has refrained MDMA from building a lot. ⚒

EMERGENCE OF CREATIVE MACHINES —

Leonel Moura

1 A complex system cannot be understood by examining its individual parts. For a complex system to produce "something", emergent properties must be present. By "something" we understand a recognisable behaviour, form or pattern in the mind of the observer. The extension of this recognition, given the state of contemporary knowledge, now largely exceeds what is usually called the visible world. The very small (such as molecules or DNA), to the very big (such as distant galaxies or black holes) are now objective parts of our world although we cannot *see* them at the level of our perceptive organs. Our world has expanded.

This kind of expansion does not affect only perception. It changes cognition. Emergence is a property of some systems that produce a higher order, a whole, based on the interaction of its simple parts. It demonstrates "how things work" beyond the simplistic mechanics of cause/effect or the linearity of procedures. Actually, emergence is the main mechanism of natural phenomena.

2 In 2003 I created the first swarm of autonomous robots able to produce original abstract paintings based on emergent behaviour. Each robot was equipped with two RGB colour detection sensors, four IR obstacle avoidance sensors, a micro-controller and two actuators, one for locomotion and the other for pen manipulation. The microcontroller was an on-board chip, to which the programme containing the rules linking the sensors to the actuators was uploaded.

The collective behaviour of the set of robots that evolved on a canvas (the *terrarium* that limited the space of the experience) was governed by the gradual increase of the deviation-amplifying feedback mechanism, and the progressive decrease of the random action, until the latter was practically eliminated. During the process, the robots showed an evident behaviour change as the result of the "appeal" of colour, triggering a kind of liveliness not observed by the viewer during the initial phase characterised by a slow random walk. This was due to the stigmergic interaction, where one robot, in fact, reacted to what other robots have done.

According to Grassé, stigmergy is the production of certain behaviours in agents as a consequence of the effects produced in the local environment by a previous action of other agents. Thus, the collective behaviour of the robots was based on randomness, stigmergy and emergence.

3 The results of these experiments demonstrate that autonomous machines can produce a *new kind of art*. This new kind of art is nonhuman in essence, as once the human operator triggers the process they lose control on the outcome. The absence of conscience, external control or predetermination, allow creative machines to engender creativity in its pure state, without any representational, aesthetic or moral flavour.

The essentials of these creations are based on the machine's own interpretation of the world and not on its human description. No previous plan, fitness, aesthetical taste or artistic model is induced. These are machines dedicated to their art.

4   In another approach, a mesh of a 3D sphere was transformed freely by a mix of algorithms, and in some cases an "ant algorithm". The initial shape went through a set of unexpected and radical changes. Holes and spikes appeared and deformations occurred. At a given moment, the process was stopped and the output sent to a 3D printer. A while later, a unique sculpture was delivered.

The essential part of this work is done by machines. My role consists in starting and finishing the process. It may seem very important, and some will see it as the inspired touch, the moment of 'true' creation, but in fact it can easily be automated. A chain of machines can be imagined, continuously creating and printing unique sculptures without human intervention.

5   Humans and machines have a common history. We can regard a sharp stone in the hands of the Paleolithic man as a machine to make engravings and trigger abstract thought. Or, consider the *camera obscura*, used by Renaissance artists as a machine to enhance realism and produce optical effects. Today, however, we have new kinds of machines that are more than mere tools. They are creative.

With the advances on artificial intelligence and bio-inspired mechanics, we can now state that some machines have a 'will' on their own. They produce things that were neither pre-determined in the algorithms nor assigned in the application design. In fact, a combination of stochastic processes and emergent behaviours can generate novelty.

This radically changes the role of humans in a creative process that involves collaborating with machines, be it a simple computer or a sophisticated robot. The man/machine collaboration is of a symbiotic kind, stemming from a constant interaction and successive positive/negative feedback from both participants. The human triggers processes but is no longer the exclusive author of the outcome. Hence, concepts need a re-evaluation. How should we redefine authorship in this new symbiotic context, since both man and machine exhibit creativeness each in their own and autonomous way?

6   Recent years have demonstrated a divide between the old humanistic vision that puts the human at the centre of all things, and increasing machine autonomy. We are witnessing an effective resistance to unavoidable cultural change. However, the endeavour to make machines more intelligent, creative and even capable of some degree of consciousness, is determined by need and is now unstoppable. We need machines to become partners and not just obedient slaves. This implies a change in machine skills, but above all in human behaviour. We need to upgrade our own contribution to the creative process. More than doing things, we should concentrate on making what does. More than manufacturing, we should focus on processes that generate an autonomous and unexpected production.

7   Art is an exceptional field for the application of these ideas. Art is experimental by nature. Architecture is another important field for change. Architecture is artificial by nature. Architecture is synthetic and increasingly determined by the extraordinary capacities machines have for visualisation and inventiveness. In particular, 3D programmes are able to generate new visions that are impossible to achieve by traditional means. And today, digital fabrication, such as in 3D printing, is able to directly build physical spaces.

An agenda for architecture should therefore be inscribed within a wider vision of the new conditions for creativity in this era of the emergence of creative machines.

In conclusion, I propose three principles for a new creativity.

1 — Embrace a symbiotic relationship with machines.
2 — Explore the power of imagination of machines.
3 — Combine all the creative processes generated by humans, other life forms and machines.

Leonel Moura is an artist engaged in applying artificial intelligence and robotics to art and design. In 2003, he created the first swarm of 'Painting Robots' able to produce original artworks. Followed by *RAP* (Robotic Action Painter, 2006), made for the American Museum of Natural History in New York, *ISU* (The Poet Robot, 2006), which writes, and *PRO* (2013), a swarm of robots that paint with the sound of music. In 2007, the Robotarium, the first zoo dedicated to robots and artificial life, opened in Alverca.

———

ZOO OR THE LETTER Z, JUST AFTER ZIONISM —

Malkit Shoshan

Nimrod was searching for a quarry. He went to the forest, looking for tracks, broken branches and droppings, trying to locate the hart, which he would ideally manage to glimpse before the chase.... Later, when the quarry could no longer run, it would turn and try to defend itself.[1]

THE AGE OF ENLIGHTENMENT[2]

The origins of both Zionism and zoos can be traced back to two revolutionary developments that came to light in the Age of Enlightenment: the classification of nature and the classification of nations. A new, obsessive interest in classifying, archiving, grouping and gathering was behind both tendencies.

Zionism, the ideology that calls for the establishment of a homeland for Jewish people, emerged in Europe during the nineteenth century, a time that was dominated by revolutionary movements. A series of national uprisings, inspired by the French Revolution, had been leading to the formation of modern Europe, with new borders delineating new nation states.[3]

The Jews were excluded from this new reality of classified territory, with its divisions according to distinctions based on race or national origin. Without a place of their own in the newly remodelled Europe, they aspired to a Jewish homeland, a nation state, where they could feel safe and free.

To the living the Jew is a corpse, to the native a foreigner, to the homesteader a vagrant, to the proprietary a beggar, to the poor an exploiter and a millionaire, to the patriot a man without a country, for all a hated rival.[4]

Leon Pinsker (Zionist pioneer)

Around the time that Zionism was gathering strength, another – seemingly unrelated – development took place: the emergence of the urban zoo. At that time, as important as nationality was the beauty of the system: science was preoccupied with classification and comparison, according to foundations laid by the likes of Linnaeus and Darwin. The first zoos, in big cities like London and Berlin, sorted animals into their families: houses of birds, reptiles, apes, and so on. The cages were highly ornamented – but aesthetically still resembled prison cells – and the various buildings, scattered pavilion-like in a garden setting, were isolated from each other. Animals were either scientifically classified objects or ornaments, or both.

THE MODERNIST ZOO

The zoo as a phenomenon continued evolving in the twentieth century. Its development can be read retrospectively as a reflective, measurable typology of the progression of society, in terms of values, applied sciences and aesthetics.

1. Nimrod, according to the Books of Genesis and Chronicles, was the son of Cush, great-grandson of Noah and the king of Shinar. He is depicted in the Tanakh as a man of power and a mighty hunter.

2. Between the fifteenth and eighteenth centuries, exotic peoples arrived in Europe. By the early nineteenth century, ethnic shows were a feature of theatre cafes. Between 1870 and the Second World War, many venues started specialising in ethnic performances, including the Crystal Palace, Barnum and Bailey in Madison Square, the Folies Bergères and the famous Panoptikum in Berlin. It was a time of professionalisation, and exotic performances morphed into mass entertainment. Reconstructed ethnic villages, zoos, colonial and international fairs, science and spectacle merged in multiple places. Exotic peoples and physical strangeness were brought together on stage as representations of the realm of abnormality.

3. Judt, Tony, *Postwar: A History of Europe Since 1945*, London: Heinemann, 2005.

4. Pinsker, Leon, *Auto-Emancipation*, 1882.

Between, and after, the World Wars the study of nature and classification became less important. Most of the natural world was already classified and whatever was not classified was considered problematic, even to the point of requiring extermination. During this period, science was predominantly about problem solving. Vaccination became prevalent and the idea of killing germs to increase health and extend life expectancy became widespread.

The physical typology of the zoo evolved as well. It became similar to an art gallery: the animals were treated almost as works of art. There were some attempts to illustrate a habitat background and occasionally to transform it into three dimensions. Carl Hagenbeck created the first cage without bars. This was the time of the rise of Modernism, of form following function; and there was a general obsessive desire to sterilise the zoo and to ensure that the exhibits were cleaned regularly. Concrete was widely used.

As environmental awareness and human rights grew in importance from the mid-twentieth century onwards, the concept of animal rights began to gain more attention. In the 1950s, psychologist Humphrey Osmond developed the concept of socio-architectural hospital design, first used in Weyburn mental hospital in 1951, based partly on Hediger's species-habitat work.[5] With advances in healthcare, animals in captivity were treated for physical and mental conditions. Zoo design started simulating the original habitat of the wild animal.[6]

CAPTIVE IN GAZA

Two white donkeys dyed with black stripes delighted Palestinian kids at a small Gaza zoo who had never seen a zebra in the flesh.[7]

Marah Land is an improvised private zoo near Gaza City. Opened by a local family, endeavouring to live in normality, it can be considered as a symbol of ordinary urban reality, a place of leisure, in the Gaza Strip. A zoo under siege, like an exotic alien, needs to re-invent itself and its resources.

CURE'E [8]

The monkeys and lions were drugged, tossed into cloth sacks and pulled through smuggling tunnels under the border between Egypt and the besieged Gaza Strip before ending up in their new homes in a dusty Gaza zoo. But to draw the crowds, what zoo manager Shadi Fayiz really wants to bring through the underground passages is an elephant. The Zoo, stocked almost entirely with smuggled animals, is a sign of Gaza's ever-expanding tunnel industry... allowing the flow of products like cigarettes, weapons and lion cubs to continue unhindered.[9]

However, for the family running the zoo in Gaza as a small business, smuggling exotic animals soon became prohibitively expensive. Imagine the zoo owners calculating the cost of smuggling a zebra – $25,000 – watched by a white donkey or two, leading naturally to the thought: why smuggle when you can DIY and dye?

Marah Land Zoo is a flashback to the Enlightenment, when cages were almost the same size as the animal and the landscape was a two-dimensional

5. Hediger described a number of standard interaction distances used in one form or another among animals. Two of these are flight distance and critical distance, used when animals of different species meet, whereas others are personal distance and social distance, observed during interactions between members of the same species. Hediger's biological social distance theories were used as a basis for Edward T Hall's 1966 anthropological social distance theories.

6. Jones & Jones architects, Seattle, is perhaps best known for pioneering the habitat immersion method of zoo design at Seattle's Woodland Park Zoo, but their work has also transformed design and scenic planning practices for highways, rivers, parks, forests, watersheds and communities.

7. Douglas, Hamilton, "Donkeys get dye-job, take on zebra role", *Reuters*, 8 October 2009.

8. The "Cure'e" is part of the hunt, as described in *The Book of Hunting* by Gaston Febus and means a *quarry* – when the animal is offered to the pack to be devoured.

9. "Lions, monkeys take underground route to Gaza Zoo", *The Jerusalem Post*, 8 August 2008.

drawing in the background. In an overcrowded environment under siege, the exotic is defined by mental creativity and physically shaped by the imagination. Marah Land's walls are painted with Disney figures, copied from smuggled, pirated, made-in-China DVDs, and with nationalist motifs that are completely decontextualised: a golden dome resembles Temple Mount but is placed in the desert like an oasis, and decorated with palm trees and donkeys.

Gaza, an oasis, used to be the place were troops and traders had easy access to water before a long march into the desert. It was also a place of learning and scholarship, and of international trade. Nowadays, Gaza is under siege and enclosed between walls, just like a forgotten paradise. [10] Its biblical beauty and its history are like a mirage that bears no relation to its current distorted mode of existence. The current reality makes its history completely unrecognisable.

Zoo, or the letter Z, just After Zionism, offers, from afar, a rare glimpse of Gaza – a view almost as exotic as the zoo animals, or the concept of a zoo itself. A glimpse of territories, people, animals under siege.

Zoo and Zionism are two phenomena that emerged out of the age of Reason, as an attempt to introduce a space for a new order for the world of things, life and culture. Sorting things out in groups, linking the similar and separating the different. The separations were not only an abstract concept. One of the consequences of this new order, was the re-organisation of space. New borders were drawn to divide nations and new cages were designed to divide animals and species from one another. The side effect of grouping the similar ended up with the exclusion of those that are different.

Now, more than a century later, we reflect on classification gone wrong, tearing apart territories and their inhabitants.

The caged donkey and the Gaza Strip represent possible consequences of classification gone wrong. The study of the boundaries that divide the world, if between nations or species, professions or programmes and touching upon a crucial topic, boundaries and border conditions, to the understanding of our living environment.

This research unfolds step-by-step the role of architecture and spatial planning in times of conflict. It takes the Israeli-Palestinian conflict as a case study in order to demonstrate how architecture can be used as both a constructive and destructive force.

10. There is a strong association between the concept of Islamic gardens and paradise. The Persian word, *pairidaeeza*, is a combination of two words that mean "surrounding wall", thus the concept of paradise is of a garden or gardens, surrounded by a wall, isolating those within and enabling them to enjoy the features established within the wall. The concept of Paradise being a garden pre-dates Islam, Christianity and Judaism by thousands of years. Originating with the Sumerians, paradise gardens were also a feature the Babylonians reserved for their gods, introducing two of what were to become basic elements of an Islamic garden: trees and water. With its adoption by the Greeks, Paradise became associated in the Abrahamic religions with Heaven.

Malkit Shoshan is an Amsterdam/New York-based architect and theorist, and founder of the Foundation for Achieving Seamless Territory. Her projects focus on the relations between architecture, planning, politics and human rights. She is the author of the award-winning book *Atlas of the Conflict: Israel-Palestine*, 2010, and of *Village*, 2014. As a guest researcher at The New Institute in Rotterdam, she is currently developing the project *Drones & Honeycombs*, on the architecture and landscape of peacekeeping missions. ✗

FUZZY PROGRAMMING IN THE ARCHITECTURAL PLANNING PROCESS —

Weimin Zhuang

English interpreter, Edward Derbyshire

A first impression is often the most telling one. You start every journey with a first step and you never forget your first kiss.
Wim Pijbes, General Director of the Rijksmuseum [1]

1. At the Rijksmuseum in Amsterdam, following a decade-long renovation project, its current curator describes how the new museum buildings have entered into use. This illustrates an important fact: the client had relatively demanding requirements for the building's location and overall feel, questions which had to be addressed prior to the architectural planning stage and preceding the architectural design.

In developing countries, many construction projects pay insufficient or no attention to planning, which means that architectural decisions not only lead to failure caused by errors in an architect's design work, but also create increasing difficulties regarding the usage and operational phases of buildings. This phenomenon is allied to a global shortage in land resources and a prevailing backlash against sustainable development. However, many developing countries have entered, or are about to enter, a stage of rapid urbanisation, and therefore a good deal of the consequent urban construction needs a theoretical and scientific basis. Construction projects, especially public urban projects, thus need to fulfil planning requirements, and the quality of planning decision-making and approval also needs to be improved. The architectural planning decision-making process can be viewed in the abstract as a process of evaluation and the acceptance and/ or rejection of a programme of implementation. The use of multiple evaluation methods has to be a particular feature of the planning decision-making process.

1. FUZZY PROGRAMMING (EPISTEMOLOGY)

The entire process of an architectural construction project, from the initial project launch and feasibility study to the architectural planning, design and construction phase, and right up to the operational stage where the building is used, is one during which there is a gradual smoothing out of any problems and research criteria. It is a process of looking for solutions and, after repeated modifications and improvements, arriving at a final resolution. When discussing the question of fuzzy programming within architectural planning, it is first of all necessary to establish the big picture concerning this complex system, in order to discover whether or not the epistemology is fuzzy and, if it is, the degree of fuzziness. Once the question of fuzzy programming within architectural planning has been seen from an epistemological viewpoint, it is then necessary to differentiate the parts of the planning process that require research based upon deterministic phenomena, and also to integrate research based upon indeterminate phenomena. In order to analyse and sort out the "both this and that" nature of indeterminate phenomena within decision-making, it is necessary to introduce fuzzy logic and fuzzy mathematical theory. [2]

2. F-logic is a type of multivalued logic; it involves a logical reasoning which is approximate rather than fixed and precise. Compared with traditional two-value logic (variables take either a true or false value) f-logic variables range between 0 and 1. The concept of f-logic has already been expanded to allow for local values, as these real values often lie in the region between completely true and completely false.

The objective of architectural planning is to gradually clarify approximate fuzzy goals that impose limits on key technical factors, thus reducing the excessive limitations on architectural forms and styles, right down to facades. Sorting out clear sociocultural goals, technological aims, usage requirements and individual dimensionality targets will delineate the architect's design objectives. Looking back to traditional architectural planning methods, the common thread is the linear thinking that continues to stress the theory of cause and effect. In contrast with developments in contemporary architectural design and theory, questions concerning historically accepted designs have become ever more numerous and complex. Given this situation, simple linear thinking can no longer solve such questions; it needs to be replenished with new methods.

Faced with the complexities of the implementation of architectural designs, research into the use of the linear thinking model for simple and partial subsystems within architectural practice *vis-à-vis* current architectural planning can seem feasible. Following on from this, the nature and law of each separate part can be added up to produce an overall nature and law, equal to the sum of all the parts. This type of approach, however, has often overlooked the specific interactions between subsystems and, even if it were to recognise the contribution to *overall quality* made by an interaction between subsystems, there might in practice remain some divisions caused by the interaction of one part with another, which gives rise to the question of considering the non-linear nature of the framework underpinning the linear superposition principle. In addition to the need to understand that the whole may not equal the sum of the parts, some flaws may remain in ensuring a specific transition from part to whole.

A more serious linear thinking process can lead to the prior assumption of a specific target for architectural planning, and the resultant accurate quantisation of capabilities can aid the realisation of this target. In such an instance one could say that linear thinking has introduced a tendency within architectural planning toward absolute, rational development. At present, architectural planning methodology still relies upon experience for crucial analytical data. However, experience has its limitations because it resides in decision-makers and specialists and is therefore relatively subjective and random as a reference standard. Owing to these deficiencies, experience has, in the past, hindered the scientific development of architectural planning methods. The field of theoretical decision-making has therefore taken a developmental path away from experience and toward science.

2. FUZZY DECISION-MAKING TOOLS (METHODOLOGY)

From the vantage point of dissimilar reflections, planning questions can be divided into systemised planning analysis, multi-category planning analysis, analysis of indeterminate conditions, digital planning and modern planning tools, etc. Of these, the "analysis of indeterminate conditions" is a difficult part of decision-making. Commonly used decision-making theory includes decisions about indeterminate conditions, risks, Bayesian decision analysis, risk preference related to utility function theory and fuzzy programming theory. The so-called indeterminate nature of information is when, as part of the decision-making process, decision-makers are faced with information that is either unclear and/or incomplete. Included in such uncertain information is the question of the decision-making event where the properties of a concept themselves appear fuzzy, which means that the construction of a fuzzy set (f-set) is required to describe the fuzzy nature of the information concerning the event.

The fuzzy programming model is initially founded upon numerous decision-making targets. As part of this model, no decision-maker can accurately define parameters, concepts or events, etc. In order to successfully handle the various relevant f-sets, they must all accumulate a series of possible choices of dissimilar confidence levels. The flexible composition of this kind of data, together with a flexibility in making choices, substantially increases this model's expressivity and adaptability. With regard to large-scale architectural planning, it is difficult to find a large number of cases which combine the multiple functions of a composite architectural system that can then be used for reference in terms of experience gained. This being the case, a prediction model can be employed to determine the situation surrounding any project. Fuzzy programming collects the relevant data and, by performing relatively simple operations, can yield comparatively realistic predictions and provide a basis for decision-makers to form judgements.

With regard to carrying forward questions of a fuzzy nature, it is relatively difficult to establish the conditions under which defined boundaries can be used. At the same time, the fuzzy programming method can be reasonably well defined, and can guarantee an increase or reduction in data control fields.

3. ARCHITECTURAL PLANNING

The emergence of mathematicised and parameterised designs, in addition to other new design methods, has supplied new architectural design methods outside the remit of the extant field of architectural design, but even more importantly, new ways of thinking about design have been introduced. In light of these architectural design methods, architectural planning looks upon historic as well as contemporary designs as mutually responsive. The range of contemporary architectural designs is no longer limited by the corpus of architectural design. The scope of architects' know-how has also expanded the bounds of previous architectural planning.

The fuzzy mathematics induced by fuzzy logic includes some extremely wide-ranging tools, among them fuzzy controls, fuzzy integrated assessment and fuzzy simultaneous equations. Fuzzy controls are used extensively in the field of engineering, and f-integrated assessments are comparatively common within management science. By combining the particular characteristics of the architectural planning process, fuzzy controls and fuzzy integrated assessments can be applied to this process.

4. CONCLUSIONS

[1] The range of contemporary architectural designs has broadened and, as such, must incorporate architectural planning.

[2] Decision-making is an essential aspect of architectural planning.

[3] Architectural planning must never be a minor consideration during the course of the construction project process.

[4] Fuzzy programming theory is very significant for architectural studies, though it presents quite substantial difficulties.

Weimin Zhuang is Dean and Professor of Architecture at the School of Architecture of Tsinghua University. He is ASC Standing Board Member, UIA Council Member and the leader of the NSFC research program, which will last from 2014 until 2017. Note: this text is part of a contribution to the NSFC research program (Architectural Programming Methodology Research in Fuzzy Decision Theory [51378275])'.

DIVERSITY MATTERS —

Sarah Lorenzen

I am the chair of an architecture programme in Southern California that focuses on first professional degrees: a five-year Bachelor of Architecture (BArch) and a three-year Master of Architecture (MArch I) for students with undergraduate degrees in fields outside architecture. Our mission statement is: "[...] To advocate for the broader purposes of architecture, including its public significance, its role in creating sustainable environments, and its provision of service to society through graduates who are responsible professionals, motivated by a sense of civic engagement". Given that we are a public institution in a highly diverse state, another essential part of our mission is to offer opportunities to minorities and economically disadvantaged students, who are poorly represented in architecture. A measure of the lack of diversity in the profession is that out of the roughly 100,000 licensed architects in the United States (20,000 of whom are registered in California), only 15 per cent are women, one per cent identify as African-American, five per cent identify as Asian and three per cent identify as Hispanic.[1]

Our undergraduate programme is, in administrative lingo, "impacted"; that is to say, many more students apply each year than can be accommodated. The average acceptance rate is around eight per cent, making ours one of the most selective architectural programmes in the country. This fact often causes surprise since we are not as well known nationally and internationally as some of the other schools in the field. The popularity of our architecture programme is in part due to its quality, and in part to the fact that we are significantly less expensive than all other architectural programmes in Southern California. The total tuition cost of a five-year BArch degree at Cal Poly Pomona is much less than one year's tuition at any of the private schools in the state. Students attending our programme are highly motivated (to be expected, given our very selective admissions policy) and they represent extremely diverse cultural, economic and ethnic backgrounds (reflective of the demographic make-up of Southern California). Half of our students are women, a third are Asian, more than a third are Latino, and most are first or second generation Americans. A large number of our students are the first in the family to go to college. A not insignificant number come from areas of the globe that are currently, or that were at the time they left, embroiled in conflict, such as Iran, Iraq, Syria, Burma, the Balkans, Vietnam and Cambodia. Others arrived in the US from Latin America with parents or grandparents who were looking to better their economic opportunities. Still others grew up affluent in the wealthy suburbs of Orange or San Diego Counties. Official statistics point to us being one of the most demographically diverse programmes in the United States.

I feel it is important to describe the profile of our programme because the culture of a school necessarily plays a part in its pedagogy, style and focus. It is also highly relevant to the issues mentioned in the *X Agendas* introductory statement, which posits that discourse *vis-à-vis* global conflict and economic inequality are as important to architecture as are formal or tectonic design concerns.

In the introduction to *X Agendas for Architecture*, the authors describe the current state of architectural professionalism as being indifferent to the cultural significance of architecture. The implication is that focusing on purely disciplinary (ie formal) concerns is shallow, or at least apolitical. Given our school's mission statement and a student population with first-hand knowledge of the "Space

1. Numbers are based on AIA membership, sourced from the AIA online article "A Snapshot of AIA Members" (as of 31 May 2011), which accounts for 80 per cent of licensed architects in the US.

of Conflict", readers of this short piece might assume that I would align myself with this critique. Simply stated, I do not. While I do not believe that there are simple causal relationships between social processes and spatial form, I do believe that the form, shape and material qualities of the built environment deeply impact society.

The focus of our programme is heavily biased towards discipline, in the most straightforward meaning of the term. We guide students to look to technique, to material and structural possibilities, to digital technology and fabrication, to the principles of sustainability, to the expressive potential of architectural representation, and to the pragmatic constraints of construction in order to generate architectural responses to particular situations. This does not mean we have surrendered "the difficult contemplation of the complexities and meanings of territorial occupation"; rather, it is through our "professional" focus that we choose to participate in these larger societal debates. To be a "professional" requires that we understand the challenges of a project and that we acquire the skills needed to respond to these challenges. Teaching architectural students to effectively learn "disciplinary" skills to produce "good" architecture is how we at Cal Poly Pomona advocate for architecture's broader purpose, its public significance, its role in creating sustainable environments and its provision of service to society.

I agree that within architecture, as in other design fields, it is increasingly difficult to offer a propitious response to a specific problem given the complex and fragmented environment within which we operate. As a response to this complex and fragmented world we find ourselves in, some architectural programmes have directed students to literally and physically represent complexity as a means of addressing the issue. Other programmes encourage students to focus on significant external aspects, such as utopian political aspirations or iconic texts, with the intention of imbuing a student's design project with deeper meaning. While these investigations can be intellectually fruitful, projects of this kind are plagued with the problem of metaphor: the project may represent the issue, but it usually fails as architecture. Another recent trend has been to turn to data-mining, assuming that given enough facts, it is possible to construct a complete view of the world in order to act upon it. Gathering large amounts of objective information can be a useful starting point, but for the data to become operational it often requires drastic oversimplification. In addition, the information collected is often uneven and subject to errors. Unlike "real" scientists (or even social scientists) who spend a substantial amount of time and effort developing controls, such as the ability to reproduce experiments, an architect's method of working is largely unverifiable conjecture. As architects, we hypothesise, speculate, surmise, guess and imagine – but there are no double-blind tests or objective measures to prove that a project will lead to a specific behaviour or set of actions. Given the rational and emotional decisions that come into play at every stage of the design process, our best choices often lie somewhere between our brain and our gut. I understand that it may be disappointing to some that we are no longer able to make grand pronouncements, but there is still great liberty in allowing architects (and architectural students) to act on a hunch, or to incrementally adjust what is already in place.

At Cal Poly Pomona we try to steer clear of dogma and certainty in approach. We work hard to give students a common professional knowledge base (including construction methods, new technologies, materiality and form-making techniques), not in order to be at the service of conventional practices, but to give students the necessary grounding for them to question, reconsider and shape architectural conventions. Students typically begin a design project by evaluating the constraints and opportunities of the "thing" they are tasked to make (typically a building, but possibly something smaller, or less concrete, or more expansive), and then to develop a physical (material) response that is appropriate to the culture(s) that the "thing" is being designed to exist within. I use the term "culture" broadly here, to include the aesthetic, material, economic and regulatory values of a place or group. The process involves having students respond to: 1) Constraints – the impact of natural laws, rules, regulations and economic realities on form; 2) Aesthetics – the significance of certain aesthetic values such as craftsmanship and representation; 3) Precedents – how certain cultures or architects have approached a particular problem in the past; and 4) Technique – following a set of graphic and/or spatial moves that yield a desirable form. In addition, students are asked to balance these disciplinary concerns with all manner of aesthetic and moral value judgments based on their own biases and those of the academic environment in which they are situated. They do all of this even while accepting that the "thing" being designed may only be tangentially connected to the internal processes and external forces that lead to its creation. Ironically, for architecture programmes known for their emphasis on form-making (many Southern California programmes fall into this group), "professionalism" is often used as a slur, synonymous with "uncreative" and "regressive", and as such something to be avoided. I see it differently: helping students to understand the cultural and aesthetic biases that shape the "profession", as well as understanding how "professional" knowledge has been constructed, is central to being able to create progressive architectural projects.

Returning to the issue of how we at Cal Poly Pomona serve our diverse student population: simply put, we teach them to be good designers. This is not only important if we want our graduates to make meaningful contributions to society; it is also an economic imperative for them. The ability to design and make beautiful "things" and to find compelling ways to represent these "things" is directly tied to their ability to gain employment. This is true anywhere, but particularly here in Southern California, given that creative endeavours are what fuel our economy. As for our lofty aim to serve society, it starts by having students understand how the culture of architecture is constructed. Aesthetics matter. Craftsmanship matters. Technology matters. Making things that are useful matters. By focusing on design we teach students to understand how the world is constructed, how it is valued and how it transforms over time. The architectural grand narrative may be dead, but in its place hundreds of unique voices have emerged. In my view, the more diverse, idiosyncratic and fragmented architectural discourse becomes, the better we will all be.

Sarah Lorenzen is a registered architect, tenured Associate Professor, Chair of the Architecture Department at Cal Poly Pomona, and Resident Director of the Neutra VDL Studio and Residences in Los Angeles. She did her undergraduate work at Smith College and at the Atlanta College of Art, and received a first professional Master of Architecture degree from Georgia Institute of Technology, and a second, post-professional Master of Architecture in Metropolitan Research and Design from SCI-Arc. ⟂

CALENDAR —
ARCHITECTURAL DIARY

Michiel Riedijk

English interpreter, Laura Vroomen

PROLOGUE

How do we interpret the concept of "development"? Is it a string of events, threaded together by day and night, the seasons, or the sun, wind and rain? Or do we become aware of developments in time only when life crosses a threshold, a rite of passage such as birth or marriage, and confronts us with sudden ruptures? The formulation of *X Agendas for Architecture* forces us to look both backwards and forwards: what continuity and ruptures can we identify in order to arrive at a greater understanding of the challenges facing architecture?

AUTUMN 2013
DIARY

What would we do without a diary? A diary contains all those things we must not forget, that must get done, be it a visit to the dentist or the purchase of a carton of milk – in short, all necessary future actions. At the same time, it does not include the really important matters because they simply cannot be forgotten: you do not jot down your children's birthdays; you know them. This makes every diary by definition ambiguous: it contains matters that are important, but not so important that we would remember them regardless.

WINTER 1986
ORGANISATION

We all had to wait in the corridor while the famous professor, smoking casually and dressed in a crisp white shirt with the top buttons undone, corrected our drawings with a few firm strokes of his red pencil. Studying at a polytechnic in a northern city in a Southern European country had a chastening effect: the floor plan, facade and section had to be organised in such a way as to naturally anchor the design in the muddy, urbanised landscape of the Po Valley. Rather than the programmatic structure or the functional analysis, it was the beauty of the artefact that mattered.

SPRING 1988
PROGRAMME

We were designing a town hall in a provincial location in the East Netherlands. The new town hall was supposed to be built beside a drab little neo-Gothic castle. The design took an oblique approach: the office part of the programme was placed in a long and narrow volume on top of a sunken, oval council chamber. The programme did not fit; the building masses clashed with the design brief. The architect we were doing our placement with, a tall man, fiercely anti-smoking, ambitious and bursting with talent, barked at us: "If it clashes, it clashes in your head". Followed by: "The programme must fit – that's all that matters."

SUMMER 1989
NARRATIVE

Art, film, ballet or literature: anything can inspire an architectural design. The gentle architect and lecturer from the south of Limburg explained to us how we could arrive at an architecture that was free from the building programme or a region's building tradition. A rigorous treatment of form, movement, sequences, colour—anything could be the guiding principle behind a design, provided the ideas solidified in architectural projections. Drawings opened up like El Lizzitsky's Prouns or Auguste Choisy's axonometrics, models could be like bas-reliefs or sculptures, as long as the sensory or haptic qualities of the narrative were given powerful expression.

AUTUMN 1992
BUILDING

The first buildings we realised were large residential blocks in former docklands or abandoned inner-city industrial estates. Building turned out to be an experience suspended between a strongly commercial culture and ambitions that reached beyond mere money and planning. The commercial culture offered us great freedom: if the design could be realised on time and within budget, all of the designers' other ambitions with regard to sustainability, dwelling types and typological experiments, for instance, would be accepted without complaint. Architectural design thrived in an era when architectural experimentation and the commercial dynamic of the construction industry were, at least in part, on the same page.

WINTER 1996
POSITION

A design is relevant only when it adopts a position in relation to the brief and the specific conditions in which it might be realised. The architect will have to learn to relate to a location or a particular cultural context by adopting a specific position. This position distinguishes the design from the gratuitous gesture or the feeble statement. The position anchors the design in a social and professional discourse, so it can be judged on its merits without critics lapsing into discussions about taste or opinion. Architecture derives its social legitimacy from the position adopted in the design.

SPRING 1998
COMPOSITION

Every design has to comply with the rules it has imposed upon itself. These rules reflect the designer's ambitions while also placing the design within the context and tradition of design. Rules are like iambic pentameters, alexandrines or the form of a sonnet, they provide structure, order and meaning. The rules ensure that the columns, panels and frames are always in the right place, regardless of programmatic contingencies or the unwieldy shape of a location. The concept of composition is an intellectual aid to prevent architecture from degenerating into an empty assemblage of components that happen to be necessary. Composition distinguishes architecture from mere building.

SUMMER 2000
MATERIALISATION

Architecture derives its power of expression from the way in which the materials used communicate the composition's position and chosen rules. The structural consistency, ie the logic with which the material elements of the design cohere, forms the cornerstone of every architectural design. Is the material distinctive? Are the seams of the structural elements lined up or not? Is the material shiny, matte, rough, smooth or quite delicate? Should we make buildings out of cardboard so they can be more easily demolished? Is materialisation just a means of expressing the position *vis-à-vis* the brief?

AUTUMN 2002
SYMBOL

It is a year after the attack on the World Trade Center and we have been invited by a large American architectural firm to be one of the five design teams for the affected site. The mayor of New York has stipulated that all the intermediate steps in the design process are to be shown in order to achieve political consensus. We propose a horizontal skyscraper as a symbol for a global, open society. The mayor wants an eye-catching tower that symbolises the power of the United States. On the plane home, we decide to withdraw from the competition.

WINTER 2006
INSTRUMENT

The director repeats his words to underline the gravity of the situation: "Failure is not an option!" On the invitation of a men's magazine, we have drawn up a design for a large casino at an out-of-the-way location on the Las Vegas Strip. The design needs to be amazing, a new paradigm in the field of gambling and hotel accommodation. After our presentation we hear no more from the client. Months later we discover that the plot and our design have been sold at many times the original value. The architecture turned out to be an instrument in a land transaction.

SPRING 2009
THE DRAWING

The *raison d'être* of the architectural profession lies in the drawing. Free from language, cultural differences or geographic peculiarities, the drawing communicates in a coded and quantifiable way an idea that can ultimately be realised in brick, timber and steel. The drawing means that the architect no longer needs to be present at the building site, and it has also resulted in increasing specialisation and division of labour within the design and construction chains. The drawing has broken the primacy of the model since a model is difficult to reproduce, and because insurance companies, developers and contractors are prepared to check drawings but not cardboard structures.

SUMMER 2010
MATTER

Architectural design is by definition 'material', although this does not necessarily mean that every single design is realised or indeed feasible. Ultimately, architecture is nothing but a material intervention in our habitat. Concepts such as space or, worse, spatiality are neither transferable nor definable. The emphasis on spatiality in education is disingenuous and leads to confusion. In short, even in its paper capacity, architecture is a material profession that needs to determine the dimension, location and nature of matter in space, since only the enclosing material can be designed and not the thing that is enclosed.

INTERMEZZO
CRAFTSMANSHIP

Architecture is a craft. Architectural design is taught in the studio. You learn to design by designing. By making a design the relationship between thought and action, reflection and practice, and position and composition is re-established again and again. This skill cannot be passed on through handbooks but must be cultivated by doing. Black lines or white paper, mass or emptiness, matter or sensory stimuli: the synthesis between these oppositions can only be brought about through designing. Designing requires practice, whereas the balance between uncompromising reality, academic thought and social status has to be re-established time and time again.

AUTUMN 2012
UTOPIA

Architecture has a utopian foundation. The architectural imagination outlines worlds that are different, perhaps better, than what we have now. By aiming for an ideal utopian situation, the design can deviate from what we already know. The design should never be based on a linear extrapolation of a found situation. Designs become meaningless if found types are repeated with impunity, or if they are based on phenomena identified through 'mapping'. The design is based on an idea, a reflection of ideals. These utopian ideals are pursued, but hopefully never achieved.

WINTER 2015
BRIEF

In the liberal arts, the design is a response to a question posed by the author or maker him/herself. Architecture is not art, it responds to questions asked by third parties. Architecture can provide accommodation and meet needs, but it is not a slave to these requirements. Architecture need not bow to the pressure of social needs, it must also be able to move and surprise by the beauty of the incidence of light, or the echoes of rapid footsteps in a stairwell. Through compositional clarity, in conjunction with a seductively powerful sensory experience, architecture can transcend everyday banality.

SPRING 2017
ACT

The architectural design will always have to bring about an improvement in the situation it finds, or else there is no point in having a design drawn up and realised in the first place. The act can be an intellectual intervention that avoids the peculiarities of the actual building process, or the social-economic dynamic in which designs come about. The design is a disposition in which matter ends up in one particular place and at no other location on earth. The designer bears a huge responsibility: only a distinctly ethical mind can prevent arbitrariness and a waste of means and space.

SUMMER 2020
CODA

The realisation of the architectural design is always set in the future; all ideas, wishes and desires are projections into the future. It is, however, impossible to know that future; chance teaches us that major or minor ruptures will inevitably force us to deviate from our planned itinerary. From flat bicycle tires to natural disasters or a financial crisis just about anything can thwart an agenda. And yet, an agenda is still necessary. Not as a social realistic blueprint or a five-year plan, but as a list of things that are quite important but would still be forgotten without a reminder.

Michiel Riedijk is principal and co-founder of Neutelings Riedijk Architects in Rotterdam and Chair of Public Building at the Faculty of Architecture, Delft University of Technology, the Netherlands.

THE CONTEMPORARY BODY OF ARCHITECTURAL EDUCATION —

Marcos Cruz

There are many different types of architecture schools today. Each has a different pedagogic vision and identity, and in some form or manner, they respond to very distinct cultural and socio-economic contexts. This variety is undoubtedly a precondition for the heterogeneous approach to architectural education that has for centuries proven so fruitful in Western architecture.

But whatever system the schools follow or advocate, the single most important factor for a good school is to guarantee a great body of teachers and students. The one is crucial in attracting the other, and that creates good work, which, in turn, appeals to the best teachers and students, and so on.... The magic synergy between tutor and student works through intense teamwork, where each project encourages a sense of exploration and is developed as a joint mission. This relationship needs to be nurtured in order to thrive. Rather than being considered as a defined structure, schools need to be hubs where students, teachers and practitioners teach and research, as well as network with others to exchange ideas. This interaction operates like an extended interface between the inner and outer world of schools, one where invention and critical thinking is able to push beyond established conventions.

The role of academic structure often tends to be overestimated, but there is indeed a major difference between a semester-based, annual or bi-annual system, and this affects the academic metabolism of a school. The semester system is typically horizontal and tends to prepare students to become "short-distance runners". The annual system, on the other hand, develops "middle-distance runners", who are often slower, but more in-depth thinkers, and whose production tends to be more personal and critical. The bi-annual system is typically vertical; it mixes students from different years and produces "long-distance runners". Their endurance is in tune with a more experimental and research-driven attitude to design, especially with projects that demand time to explore unknown territories. Not surprisingly, many students of this system are inclined at some point in their career to become engaged in academic activities.

The majority of schools continue to rely on what I call a "universal knowledge-curriculum", forcing students through too many subjects with the aim of giving them a conceptual overview, which in the end is generalist in terms of design, history, technology, and social and environmental studies. Only a minority of schools offer a more focused, student-tailored curriculum. At a time when advances in technology are moving extremely quickly, and information technologies enable knowledge to be available more or less everywhere instantaneously, this is certainly a worthwhile approach. I like to think of schools having less curriculum and more hands-on experimentation, and, like a contemporary skin, to be more permeable to a free flow of information, avoiding a self-contained and over-regularised system in favour of a far simpler and more open network. In this regard, a design-integrated and design-focused pedagogic model can run parallel to optional open classes, with core subjects strategically coordinated (and even integrated) with design.

Critical in this context is the enduring role of the design studio. It is worth questioning how contemporary studios are effectively offering a specialised, yet also multi-layered education in architecture. How do we teach design in a way that considers a multiplicity of fields (conceptual, methodological, historical, socio-political, technological, etc), and how is the vital role of applying knowledge through the use of contemporary design tools preparing our students differently for the profession of tomorrow? The contemporary studios are the students' homes, they are the inhabitable inner 'flesh' of architecture schools – intimate places where students interact and communicate, and from where they tailor their courses to their preferences and interests, enabling them to create their own trajectory of learning. From the extreme size of an open-plan environment to the extreme subdivision of the space allocated to individual units, an array of different areas and atmospheres is possible. Whatever the type available, what is fundamental is that students are able to work at school in surroundings that promote a culture of creative dialogue, teamwork and critical debate. I have argued in previous articles that contemporary students are like "networked virtuosos" who operate in media studios as highly skilled masters of their craft, and who increasingly network with a worldwide community of experts outside the studio. Beyond the much-discussed change from the drawing board to the computer interface, today's new processes require new work environments. New computational tools are triggering original modes of production and fabrication, allowing students to test more complex geometries and tectonics in a three-dimensional and material way. This fosters a much more intimate relationship between the act of designing and physical/spatial production. As a consequence, research centres are appearing all over the world where studios and workshops are merging into innovative work environments. All this is possible due to the fact that contemporary schools are acquiring increasingly sophisticated equipment that facilitates collaboration between architectural schools and leading industrial partners.

This shift also announces a clear path towards much more collaborative work procedures in both academia and professional practice. Unlike the old model where a modernist master was able to dictate almost entirely the design of a building, contemporary students are part of a collective of experts and consultants that create a multi-layered and inter-disciplinary sociality, in which many people take part.[1] An intensified design-through-making attitude is becoming increasingly relevant in schools. Until the 1990s, ideas and concepts were the driving force of architectural experimentation and innovation, whereas today the focus is ever more frequently driven by the possibilities of materialised thought. The technical means available allow us to go beyond the illustration of ideas to actual physical demonstrations, which is why understanding materials and tools is becoming so pertinent. 1:1 prototyping is an essential way forward for students to learn how to apply their tools and techniques to spaces that are not only optimised and efficient, but also socially and poetically meaningful.

However, due to this growing reliance on new tools of fabrication, contemporary schools are more than ever in need of an experimental attitude to compensate for an otherwise excessively technique-reliant approach. The experiential and practical sensory engagement with materials and space needs to precede the conceptual understanding of it. This has, for example, made us in Unit 20 at the Bartlett change our work method in the last few years, so that students now initiate their year with a material investigation that is digitally fabricated, while at the same time establishing the overall research premises of their design. Important here is that architecture students require a much more in-depth sensibility toward materials and craft at a time when there are so many new technologies and material composites being developed, combined with the acute need for a sustainable approach to our built environment. It is often shocking to realise how limited the

1 . Maffesoli, Michel, *The Time of the Tribes: The Decline of Individualism in Mass Society*, London: Sage, 1996. Original title *Le Temps des Tribus*, Paris: Meridiens Klincksieck, 1988.

material vocabulary of students still is, and how much this impoverishes the haptic and environmental dimension of what they propose.

In summary, there are key aspects relevant to a contemporary body of architectural education, which include distinctive physical surroundings, personalised studios and well-equipped workshops (including laboratories for bio-technological and environmental research). This body requires a simplified curriculum where design research has a central role, and where a multi-annual pedagogic structure offers students more time to develop their work in a tailored and more collaborative way. Contemporary schools of architecture are places that are therefore tending to follow a more research-by-design model, providing students with both analytical and critical instruments for engaging with physical prototyping. Beyond visualisation, this allows for materialised thought that is able to connect more directly with society.

Finally, I would like to refer to the importance of "lateral thinking", as a vital method of creative problem solving.[2] I extrapolate it to the idea of "lateral design" as a quintessential method that students use to find new answers in an increasingly complex world – one that is environmentally unbalanced, has limited resources, is financially volatile and whose societies are undergoing profound change. There is a need today for more non-linear thinking systems that do not seek obvious and predictable outcomes. The notion of "lateral" implies thinking "out of the box", combined with more synthetic action that is likely to generate creative ideas across a variety of disciplines by exploring intuitive, rather free-flowing design possibilities. In this context, there is a real need for schools to encourage a greater risk-taking attitude in students, allowing them to 'fail' rather than only pushing them to succeed.

Contemporary schools are like the contemporary body. They are network bodies in which the scattered nature of their parts promotes a direct engagement with society by means of advanced technology. With their highly equipped design-studio workshops, they look less like the classical model of an art school, or the functionalistic matrix of a purpose-built modernist building, and more like the monstrous set-up found in sci-fi movies, where robotic armatures and bio-technical 3D printing equipment allow for an unprecedented production of objects and prototypes.

As teachers and leaders of architectural schools today, we need to anticipate the anatomy of these schools and consider how to prepare future architects so that they will be able to act in a very different world from ours. To achieve this, it is vital to help students to develop a "growth mindset", not only by teaching them the most advanced skills, but also by triggering their sense of openness and readiness to embrace novelty and change.[3] More than ever, our contemporary students need to know how to learn in order to be able to respond to the unpredictability of forthcoming challenges. We need to embrace the contemporary body of architectural education, stimulate new collaborative work and innovative forms of practice, and make our students pro-active by giving them the scope and courage to develop their own architectural identity and thoughts. Ultimately, we need to awaken their inner dreams as architects, and give them through the education of today the tools to realise the architecture of tomorrow.

2. de Bono, Edward, *Lateral Thinking: A Textbook of Creativity*, London: Penguin, 2009.

3. Dweck, Carol, *Mindset: How You Can Fulfil Your Potential*, London: Robinson, 2012.

Marcos Cruz is a practising architect and co-founder of the atelier marcosandmarjan. He is a reader at the Bartlett School of Architecture, where he was the director between 2010 and 2014. His varied teaching activities as an investigator, tutor and critic have been carried out in numerous international universities, including the University of Westminster, UCLA and IAAC, but most of all at University College London where he has been running MArch Unit 20 for over 15 years and teaching BiotA/rC7. He is also co-editor of the Syn.de.Bio online forum, while his investigations into Neoplasmatic Architecture won the RIBA President's Award for Outstanding Research in 2008. Cruz has published numerous books, among them *The Inhabitable Flesh of Architecture*, 2013; two annual *Bartlett Books*, 2012/2013; *AD – Neoplasmatic Design*, 2008; *marcosandmarjan – Interfaces/Intrafaces*, 2005 and *Unit 20*, 2002. ✕

THE ONLY CONSTANT —
THE AGENDA OF ARCHITECTURE

Pnina Avidar

> Architecture in its truest sense may not be academically
> defined. If it is, it becomes a dead, non-growing entity
> of styles or cliché.
>
> John Lautner [1]

1 . Quotation by Frank Escher in *John Lautner, Architect*, Frank Escher ed, Basel: Birkhäuser, 1998.

2 . "No other major profession is so often seized with worry about its own future as is architecture. The reason for the concern is substantial, given several factors about the field. For example, some of its work can be handled by other professions, such as engineers or interior designers. The demand for architectural services is unusually influenced by fluctuations in economic conditions. Other parties in the building industry limit much of the architect's authority, even when she has good jobs. A further complication is that within architecture itself, criteria of fashionable design change frequently." *Architecture from the Outside In: Selected Essays by Robert Gutman*, Dana Cuff and John Wriedt eds, New York: Princeton Architectural Press, 2010, p 33. Essay first published in May 1977.

3 . Forty, Adrian, *Words and Buildings: A Vocabulary of Modern Architecture*, London: Thames and Hudson, 2004, p 14.

4 . *Rethinking Architecture: A Reader in Cultural Theory*, Neil Leach ed, London: Routledge, 1997.

5 . http://danariely.com.

6 . Forty, *Words and Buildings*, p 13.

Architecture makes sense of the world in various ways, offering signification, reason and sensation. As such, the concern with the future of architecture and the role of the architect in it is more than a mere habit, it is a cyclic ritual, a perpetual need that is rooted in the *nature* of architecture itself. [2] Within the scope of this essay, and in order to reflect on the agenda of architecture, I will look at the *nature* of architecture through the magnifying glass of the language used in the architectural discourse. To be more precise, I will make a brief comparison of words used in architectural debates during the modern and contemporary periods, as well as considering their collective meaning.

Both architecture and language can be seen as symbolic systems that communicate meaning and are subjected to particular prevailing conventions at any given point in time. [3] The *nature* of architecture is then "the product of a way of thinking" that touches on metaphysics (time, space and being), deals with the physicality of life, and, in the process of its realisation, engages with prevailing beliefs (economics, politics, religion etc). [4]

Architecture inevitably deals with a possible future that is based on a current premise. Hence, setting up an agenda for architecture or considering what architects should do involves foresight and calls for a prognosis. The act of "reading" the future is a venture. As Dan Ariely explains, our comprehension of the world is limited since a) we cannot regard all possible alternatives, b) we have certain habits in our way of seeing the world and a set of personal presuppositions, and c) we are highly influenced by the preferences of our surroundings. [5] Taking into consideration these limitations, I will employ the words used to describe the actuality of architecture in order to point out and to determine its agenda.

Language, once seen as an insufficient medium for communicating architecture, is now filling numerous books on architectural production, history, theory, architects' biographies, exhibitions and their catalogues, architecture Internet sites, TV programmes, architectural education publications and more. [6] Communicating architecture through language has become a vital necessity for the architect, a fact that is evident when looking into the curricula of architecture schools and the courses that are being offered to practising architects via architects' unions. Architects are required to be able to pitch their ideas as fast as possible and to mould them into a consumable and easy to digest form.

In this regard, a brief comparison between the vocabulary used in the modern architectural debate and the one used in the contemporary debate clearly demonstrates the transformation architecture is undergoing. If the language of modern architecture consisted of words such as "form, function, space, design, order, structure" and so forth, we now find they have been replaced by "geometries, urgency, networking, strategy, generic, innovation" and many more. [7]

7. Forty, *Words and Buildings*, p 19.

Looking at the collective meaning of the words above points out that modern architecture dealt with and communicated within reasonably defined physical boundaries rooted in philosophy and the arts. Modern architecture was therefore a part of a world that could be ordered and structured; it functioned within a context, it related to history and was transparent and true.

Subsequently, architecture altered into a discipline that now defines itself as an abstract field of action anchored in economics and politics. Contemporary architecture is part of a world of multiplicity, it operates within global regions and is subjected to bottom-up initiatives and accelerating technological developments.

The contemporary vocabulary of architecture discusses processes. The contemporary vocabulary of architecture cannot but encompass change. Architecture replaces the permanent with the variable and therefore has to address the system and not the object. Architecture has shifted from the constant to the temporary, replacing the solid with the ephemeral.

Consequently, the agenda for architecture has to deal with change as the base concept for thought and action since "All fixed, fast-frozen relations, with their train of ancient and venerable prejudices and opinions, are swept away, all new-formed ones become antiquated before they can ossify. All that is solid melts into air, all that is holy is profaned, and men at last are forced to face... the real conditions of their lives and their relations with their fellow men". [8]

8. Berman, Marshall, *All That is Solid Melts Into Air: The Experience of Modernity*, New York: Simon and Schuster, 1982, p 21.

When *the only constant is change*, the architect's merit is "... the ability to hold two opposed ideas in the mind at the same time", to navigate between (often conflicting) scales, worlds and disciplines, and to consolidate them all into a whole. [9] Architecture as we know it comes to an end, and in order to obtain its signifying role it becomes a diverse condition. Within that condition, architecture can concurrently be considered as an art, a science, a profession, a character, a style, an action, a methodology, a strategy, a practice, a field, the process and the product.

9. "Before I go on with this short history, let me make a general observation — the test of a first-rate intelligence is the ability to hold two opposed ideas in the mind at the same time, and still retain the ability to function. One should, for example, be able to see that things are hopeless and yet be determined to make them otherwise." *The Crack-Up* by Scott Fitzgerald, F. Originally published as a three-part series in the February, March and April 1936 issues of *Esquire*, http://www.esquire.com/features/the-crack-up.

Architecture, then, is the result of a rigorous examination and iterative experiments, and not the validation of preconceived hypotheses. Architecture circumscribes spatial transformations that resonate within a spatial canon, transformations that are connected to a physical awareness and which accommodate various and constantly changing emerging needs.

When the *only constant is change,* the architect can be the Massive Changer, the Civic Activist, the Contractual Innovator, the Near Future Inventor, the Strategic Designer, the Management Thinker, the Community Enabler, the Professional Generalist, the Public Intellectual, the Educator of Entrepreneur, the Whole Earth Architect, the Double Agent, the Historian of the Present, the Editor of the Beyond or the Environmental Medic. [10] Architecture is in that case an entrepreneurial condition creating its own demand and defining the spatial challenges that lie ahead.

10. Hyde, Rory, *Future Practice: Conversations from the Edge of Architecture*, New York/London: Routledge and Taylor & Francis, 2012.

In conclusion, change as an underlying notion entails architecture's present need to develop its own change-vocabulary, change-values and change-intelligence as a means to support its power of conveying meaning and making sense.

Pnina Avidar is engaged in architectural research & design — 12PM-Architecture (owner), architecture education (Head of the Architecture Department at MA&U Tilburg) and architectural writing (articles in various media and past editor of OASE). Pnina is... an ephemeral condition.

DIGITALLY-DRIVEN EXPERIMENTATION IN ART AND ARCHITECTURE –

Henriette Bier

1 . Benjamin, Walter, "The Work of Art in The Age of Mechanical Reproduction", 1936.

2 . Manovich, Lev, *The Language of New Media*, Cambridge, MA: The MIT Press, 2001.

3 . Carpo, Mario, *The Alphabet and the Algorithm*, Cambridge, MA: The MIT Press, 2011.

4 . De Landa, Manuel, Deleuze and the Use of the Genetic Algorithm in Architecture, *Architectural Design: Contemporary Techniques in Architecture*, Ali Rahim ed, New York: Wiley, 2002.

5 . Bier, Henriette, et al, Building Relations", *The Architectural Annual 2005– 2006*, H Bekkering and D Hauptmann eds, Delft University of Technology, Rotterdam: 010 Publishers, 2007.

6 . Bier, Henriette, and Terry Knight, "Digitally-Driven Architecture", H Bier and T Knight eds, *Footprint*, 6, Delft University of Technology, 2010, pp 1–4.

7 . Bier and Knight, "Digitally-Driven Architecture", 2010, pp 1–4.

Walter Benjamin stated in 1936 that mechanical reproduction has freed the work of art from its dependence on ritual, which implied, among others, a move from drawing towards photography and film. [1] In an even more extreme process of emancipation, digital production implies among others that the work of art and architecture become digital, and therefore address such principles as numerically controlled computer representation, generation, production and operation. [2] Thus, as Carpo convincingly argued more recently, the historical understanding of buildings as physically built, identical replicas of architectural intent (formalised in design), which in the twentieth century became serially mass-produced identical copies, is challenged by contemporary digitally-driven parametric multiplicity and variation. [3] Such multiplicity and variation, which allows versions of architectural intent to be physically implemented and experienced through, for example, spatial reconfiguration, has been analogously explored within the Border Conditions (BC) studio, with the understanding that multiple versions of the built space may be achieved through kinetic transformation.

Furthermore, experimentation with parametric multiplicity and variation was also addressed in *X Agendas for Architecture*, 2011, organised by the BC studio, with a focus on generative design and digitally-driven production. These were presented and discussed as tools for investigating not only an array of digital techniques, but also for critically revealing what these techniques might offer architectural and artistic production, as well as outlining the challenges that remain in their application. The relationship between generative processes and the digitally-driven production of 3D artefacts and 2D drawings was addressed by Marta Malé-Alemany through architectural design and fabrication experiments with customised robotic devices, while Leonel Moura presented Robot Art.

Digitally-driven, generative design processes have been a focus of current artistic and architectural research and practice largely due to the phenomenon of emergence explored within self-organisation, which is defined as a process in which the organisation of a system emerges bottom-up from the interaction of its components. [4] Self-organising swarms, for instance, are employed in generative design processes that deal with large amounts of data, which at times may feature conflicting attributes and characteristics. [5] These attributes and characteristics are incorporated into behaviours where design components, such as programmatic units, swarm towards targeted spatial configurations. [6] In this context, architectural design becomes procedural rather than object-oriented, and architectural form emerges from a process in which the interaction between all parts of the system generates the result. Thus the architect or artist becomes the designer of the process, but only indirectly of the result.

Basically, swarms operate as multi-agent systems consisting of simple agents that interact locally with one another and their environment, based on simple rules, which lead to the emergence of complex, global behaviour. [7] Their use in design is of relevance because of their ability to embody both natural (human) and artificial (design-related) aspects. Basically, swarms are set up as parametric models, which incorporate characteristics and behaviours that represent the natural and artificial systems, whereas simulations of behaviours show the operation of such systems in time.[8]

Like natural agents, intelligent (artificial) agents are conceived (in computer science) as autonomous entities able to perceive through sensors and act upon an environment using actuators.[9] Interactions between human and artificial agents may follow principles as described in the Actor–Network Theory (ANT), implying that material-semiotic networks are acting as a whole, whereas the clusters of actors or agents involved in creating meaning are both material and semiotic.[10] ANT, therefore, entails the agency of both humans and non-humans, although agency is not located in either one or the other, but in the heterogeneous associations between them.

Such heterogeneous, generative processes implemented in simulations are extensively discussed by De Landa in relation to his interpretation of Deleuze's idea that form emerges from within matter itself, hence a philosophy of immanence (not transcendence) in which matter itself has the capacity to generate form through immanent, material, morphogenetic processes.[11] In this context, simulations based on cellular automata and multi-agent systems are defined as forms of knowledge visualisation, and a means for conceptualising spaces that emerge from local, bottom-up interactions.

Simulation in relationship to art and architecture has been discussed within *X Agendas for Architecture* with respect to the ability it has to support the generative development of artistic and architectural production. As De Landa argues, digitally-driven production processes and their intrinsic connection to physical, mathematical, biological and other sciences are enabling art and architecture to go beyond a mere technological application, in order to address systems, population and topological thinking. While system thinking implies that all parts of a system are to be understood in relation to each other,[12] population[13] replaces typological thinking as it rejects the focus on representative types and instead emphasises individual variation, while topology[14] studies space and transformation.

In this context, the artist and architect develop (virtual and physical) agents that produce artworks and architectural artefacts, thus artistic and architectural production becomes the result of multiple, interacting natural (human) and artificial agents.[15] Such agent-based processes imply that under similar conditions, identical or similar (virtual and physical) agent systems can produce multiple (or endless) variations of artworks or architectural artefacts due to the emergent properties of the system.

Natural and artificial agents therefore operate as actors involved in creating meaning at both a material and semiotic level, while humans represent only one of many possible agential embodiments. This understanding relies on De Landa's neo-materialist cultural theory, which rejects the dualism between nature and culture, matter and mind, natural and artificial; instead, reality is revealed in material, self-organised processes. In this context, and in opposition to Alberti's formalisation of (notational and authorial) architectural representation consisting of plans, elevations and sections from which materialisation is implemented, multiple and various architectural materialisations emerge today from interactions between (natural and artificial) agents, while authorship becomes hybrid, collective and diffuse.[16]

Thus notions such as original, copy, production and reproduction are subject to redefinition. If the tool that was used to create in the age of mechanical reproduction (the pen) differs from the machine used to make copies today (the printer), these tools conflate into one, computer-numerically controlled system, blurring not only the distinction between original and reproduction, but

8. De Landa, "Deleuze and the Use of the Genetic Algorithm in Architecture", 2002.

9. Russell, Stuart J and Peter Norvig, *Artificial Intelligence—A Modern Approach*, Upper Saddle River NJ: Prentice Hall, 2003.

10. Latour, Bruno, *Reassembling the Social: An Introduction to Actor-Network-Theory*, Oxford: Oxford University Press, 2005.

11. Russell and Norvig, *Artificial Intelligence*, 2003.

12. Latour, *Reassembling the Social*, 2005.

13. Mayr, Ernst, "Darwin's Influence on Modern Thought", 1999, retrieved from http://www.biologie.unihamburg.de/bonline/e36_2/darwin_influence.htm.

14. Sierpinski, Waclaw, *General Topology*, Mineola, NY: Dover Publications, 2012.

15. Moura, Leonel and Henrique Garcia Pereira, *Symbiotic Art Manifesto*, 2004, retrieved from http://www.lxxl.pt/artsbot/.

16. Carpo, *The Alphabet and the Algorithm*, 2011.

17. Sierpinski, *General Topology*, 2012.

also between representation and generation, due to the processes through which physically built space is produced and utilised. [17] Multiplicity and variation therefore imply not only that design or art emerge from local interactions between non-human and human agents, but also that physically built space which incorporates computer-numerically controlled (non-human) agents adapts and reconfigures in response to human needs.

While art and architecture increasingly incorporate aspects of non-human agency by employing information and knowledge contained within the (worldwide) network that connects electronic devices, the relevant question is not whether interactive, reconfigurable environments can be built, but how (artificial) intelligence can be embedded into environments in order to serve everyday life. In this context, digitally-driven art and architecture are not only produced (created or designed and fabricated) by digital means but actually incorporate digital, sensing-actuating mechanisms that allow them real-time operation and interaction with environments and users. [18]

18. Bier and Knight, "Digitally-driven Architecture", 2010.

In the last decade, digitally-driven architecture aimed at tentatively answering the question of how (artificial) intelligence could be embedded into environments in order to serve everyday life through enabling real-time interaction between natural or artificial environments and users. The assumption that digitally-driven building components (such as doors, walls, floors, etc) may offer solutions for dealing with the rapid increase of population and urban densification, as well as the contemporary inefficient use (25 per cent) of built space, was explored by introducing spatial reconfiguration, which is enabling multiple, changing uses within reduced time frames. Furthermore, the advancement of embedded, interactive or robotic energy and climate control systems which employ renewable energy sources, such as solar and wind power, aims to reduce architecture's ecological footprint while enabling a time-based, demand-driven use of space.

In this context, notions such as "process-based" and "time-based" may require further definition since they address, respectively, not only the production, but also the operation of architecture. If design becomes process-oriented rather than object-oriented, then the use of space becomes time-based rather than programme-based, which implies that architects increasingly design processes, while users operate multiple, time-based architectural configurations emerging from the same physical space. Similarly to process-based artistic experimentation, digitally-driven architecture exploits emergent results from interactions between human and non-human agents. However, digitally-driven architecture aims to exploit emergent phenomena not only at the design and production level, but also at the operational level, where users contribute to the emergence of multiple architectural configurations.

Henriette Bier has worked with Morphosis (1999–2001) on internationally relevant projects in the US and Europe and has taught computer-based architectural design (2002–2003) at universities in Austria, Germany and the Netherlands. Since 2004 she has taught and researched at the Delft University of Technology with focus on experimental applications of digital technologies in architectural design and architecture. In 2008 she finalised her PhD on System-embedded Intelligence in Architecture and results of her research are published internationally and have been presented in books, journals, symposia and conference proceedings. ⚓

LE PARI(S) DE BKK —

François Roche

English interpreter, Camille Lacadée

1. In Dan Simmons' novel *Hyperion*, the transdoor is a vector of physical translation.

2. The city is covered by $CO+CO_2$ particles that filter the light through spectral frequencies of grey, creating a glossy, luminous, vaporous, pheromonal, hideous, shaded, transpiring, cottony, rugged, dirty, hazy, suffocating, hairy grey atmosphere that both reveals the degree of pollution and wraps the city in an extremely sophisticated coat, as the witness of ambivalence to the situation.

3. On the one hand, the bottom-up, under the freeway... a self-organised, "messy", excessively rustling human zone, where frictions and encounters are intrinsically implemented, embedded... a potential of adaptability, transformability, tolerance and indeterminism... from the shapelessness of the city to human pathologies and improvisations... where everything is dedicated to the logic and illogic of the swarm... in the dynamism of the exchanges, in the smelled, swallowed, digested, shitted substances, in the confusion between the taste of stir-fried food, the fragrance of rain on asphalt... the dirtiness and the beauty in the hell of human energies and vitalism.... On the other hand, the top-down, the freeway... a disseminated downtown dedicated to its own representation, its self-satisfaction with its emergence in the sky, which embodies the running of the financial ideology through multiple condominiums of personal social "successes", stacked and disconnected from each other... both *alive and dead*: alive through the endlessly upward high-rising of the city, with numerous sites under construction, symbolising the activity, working potential and efficiency of the economic model; and simultaneously dead for the same reasons, especially when the condos are completed... then working as financial products more than as actual living places. The freeways, organised as a gigantic, octopus-like network floating in the urban tissue, are the "horizontal" line separating and distinguishing these two types of human habitudes of self-representation or social strata... enabling a myriad of connections, flirts, touches, caresses and collision points between the two.

(... BETTING ON BKK/)

Charles de Gaulle Airport (CDG) is a transactional transitory zone, a transdoor opening to a parallel, simultaneous, negotiable universe....[1] The escape it offers may be narrow, it's wonderful anyway... just right for a native emigrant.

Every other week at least over the last ten years, in order to extricate myself from the museum city, frozen, transfixed in its smothering conservatism and pedantic degradation... CDG Airport Terminal 1.... "Beam me up, Scotty".

BKK/

The dust enshrouds the city and its biotope, modifies its climate.... Within this fog of specks and particles, Bangkok turns into a melting pot of hypertrophic human activity, of convulsive exchanges of energy.[2] At the antipode of the canons of modern urbanism and its panoply of instruments of prediction, planning and determinism, the city of Bangkok, ectoplasmic, is conceived in between aleatory rhizomes where the arborescent growth is at the same time a factor of its transformation and its operational mode....[3] It is an urban environment made of protuberances and emergences, where capitalist merchandise flows through a profusion of gigantic, aseptic, cold and deterritorialised malls, immersed in an intoxicating urban chaos.

Le pari(s) de BKK is a mixture of dirtiness and beauty, of metabolism and verticality, of traffic jams and smashed-flat motorcycles that swiftly find their way through, of fly-over concrete-bridge-networks snaking their trajectories through a stochastic urbanism with a permanent confusion, indistinction, de-identification between publicness and privacy, exhibitionism and intimacy, repulsion and magnetism.... It is an apparatus (and not a display) whose emergences do not pretend to be long lasting or eternal.... Surviving, dying, resurrecting, dying again in a logic of contingency and vitalism, the logic of a palpitating organism stuttering between life-and-death drives, Eros and Thanatos... a second nature where the urban tissue is alive, and where the city is not limited and framed by its "representation", not frozen into a normative and panoptical system of survey and representation....

Le pari(s) de BKK is an inter-zone where the possible is uncertain and the impossible plausible... an ad hoc principle of urban (un)planning....

STUTTERING/

In the hotchpotch entanglement of flux, friction, trifle and cum, a few spots sparkle, ingrain, identify themselves as the temples of normalised shopping mall exchanges: Terminal 21, Siam Paragon, MBK, Emporium, Gateway, Future Town, Central World, Robinson, plus a handful always under construction, like La Samaritaine, Galeries Lafayette, BHV-Bazar Napoléon or Bon Marché in Paris.... These nineteenth century temples of commerce work under ritualised transactional modes as the first penitentiary worlds of exchange, socialised and hierarchical biospheres from the cashier to the department head, where the customer, machine subject and object of desire, is able to exercise the fiction of their power, of their supposed *jouissance*, where the climate as well as the ambulatory and relational social modes are codified, formatted and artificialised as the counterpoint to the swarming and untameable city blighting its accesses.... But in Paris these capitalised zones have malevolently turned inside out, and the city itself is now confused with their merchandised display, originally limited, contained and recognisable within geographic (id)entities....

Paris and BKK, two points on the planet, two asymmetrical evolutions, as if following two divergent, contingent space-time cynosures... one confusing the client with the citizen, the other still relying on the original contradiction between the object and the "subject" of capitalism. [4]

Let us not be mistaken.... This is not so much an opposition between two cities as it is an opposition between several temporalities: Le pari(s) de BKK is the Paris of a future anterior eviscerated of all nostalgia, projecting a time when the city was not (yet) conditioned by the subordination of the little bourgeois Ecolo plugged into their iPod mini, on a Velib ride, whatever their origins, education, salary and gender, to a standardisation of appearances... free-willingly becoming the symptom of a global intellectual fraud.

SCHIZOID APPARATUSES/

What perhaps is most relevant in Le pari(s) de BKK is the potential confrontation between the antagonistic forces of two urban models, a permanent union and divorce of the "Commune and the Capital", intrinsically intertwining to generate a systemic live output.

The first model is made of the sound of the human swarm, musical and terrestrial, on the city's ground, and includes permissiveness of transformation, adaptation, graft and necrosis on its first four to five floors from the ground... where one can erect, destroy, alter, gangrene and nest one's familial, commercial or amicable system without having to report to a public authority, as if in the midst of a judicial vacuum.... The other is looking down on the first, appearing as a skyline, a vertical succession of malls, condos and hybrids... emerging without creating any centralised downtown, subject to opportunities, speculations and resistances... themselves subject to strict rules of materiality, normality and global representational aesthetics. [5]

Le pari(s) de BKK is this caress, rustle, friction territory.... It makes the encounter possible between the one who only exercises their power through the compulsive merchandise of turnkey life models, and the one who, conversely, is in synchronicity with the animal pleasure of things and beings, smells and sounds, illusions and ripe fruits.... One makes a skyline, the other humming asphalt.... One is capitalising their economy by freezing it in the standardisation of an imaginary vertical home (a condo 70 per cent unoccupied, like so many financial products where habitability is a fiction), a producer but not a consumer of a horizontal urban line, a financial transfer zone.... The homogenisation of desires and satisfaction allows for the flow of merchandise and the circulation of the money-narrative (the city has turned into a transactional economic vector), which disincarnates in the construction of pseudo-luxurious, pseudo-comfortable, pseudo-designed, pseudo-inhabited, speculated and volatile products in a skylinisation process... before the bursting of the financial bubble into a myriad of collateral effects, junk bonds and fatal contingencies.... [6] The predictable deorganisation of profits....

4. "Subject" here refers to a subordinate, as in a king's subject.

5. 100 high-rise buildings are currently planned and/or are under construction in Bangkok.

6. "Capitalism is nearly indifferent to the contents of the stories of which it enables the circulation. The money-narrative is its canonical story because it brings together its two properties: it tells us that we can tell any stories we like, but that the stories' profits must return to their author, or at least to those who convey their narratives (green washing, social washing, security washing)". Lyotard, Jean-François, *Instructions Païennes*, Paris: Éditions Galilée, 1977.

_acan, Jacques, _Le séminaire,_
7, L'éthique de la psychanalyse
_9–1960_, Paris: Seuil, 1986.

Paris is used like a beta
elopment zone for the
ury industry. International
gazines often depict Paris
a place where people
the street look like fashion
dels, provoking the
is Syndrome: a transient
chological disorder
countered by tourists
ting Paris, and Japanese
tors in particular. It is
racterised by a number
psychiatric symptoms such
acute delusional states,
llucinations, feelings of
secution (perceptions
being a victim of prejudice,
gression or hostility
m others), derealisation,
personalisation, anxiety
d also psychosomatic
nifestations such as
ziness, tachycardia and
eating. See "Paris Syndrome",
ipedia, http://en.wikipedia.
/wiki/Paris_syndrome.

The other has nothing to capitalise except its daily ritornello of "difference and repetition" in an erotic, pornographic rustle conditioning; as Lacan wrote: "the epidermal contact, complete, total, between the body and a world itself open and quivering [...] from a touch, and at the horizon, a lifestyle of which the poet shows the way and the direction".[7]

Le pari(s) de BKK stutters on two models of jouissance, between the city-as-product-of-the-capital and the city-that-doesn't-give-a-shit, busy as it is getting pleasure from it, in the superimposition of two strata, two morphologies, two mechanics of nonlinear exchanges.... But Paris only has one model left: the human bourgeois, or bourgeois-becoming, insulated in their soundproofed home, listening for the least untimely noise that might get through the partition walls to immediately denounce it, confusing life with its representation... with its corollary of sadness and its dependency on the display organised by the central system of power delegation, the political, social, monarchical operator: la Mairie de Paris.[8]

On the other side, BKK, where two stories of time are still plausible.... Like an urbanism for Schrödinger's cat, it is simultaneously dead and alive, a contingency, a place of parallel stories... exuding the possibility to navigate in their frictions, the crib of their folds and of generated possibilities, without subscribing to the one or the other as the unique mode of existence....

The jump has been made.... One year ago.... Le pari(s) de BKK... Could it be only a 14-hour flight, a glass of whisky, three meals, two movies, some writing and half a drawing away...? A normalised distance... linear... almost disappointing... inasmuch as one carries one's psyche in one's baggage... and the distance travelled will not metabolise its dependencies....

François Roche is the principal of New-Territories (R&Sie(n) / [eIf/bʌt/c]). He is based mainly in BKK, often in NY and no more in Paris. Through these different structures, his architectural works and protocols seek to articulate the real and/or fictional, the geographic situations and narrative structures that can transform them. www.new-territories.com

———————

TACTICS OF THE MIDDLE —

Toomas Tammis

In the middle, where nothing is supposed to be happening, there is almost everything. And at the extremes — which according to the moderns house the origin of all forces, Nature and Society, Universality and Locality — there is nothing except purified agencies that serve as constitutional guarantees for the whole.[1]

Bruno Latour

1 . Latour, Bruno, *We Have Never Been Modern*, Catherine Porter trans, Cambridge, MA: Harvard University Press, 1993, p 123.

Estonia is a border condition par excellence. Geographically and historically it is on the border of Europe and Russia. Economically, it changed from capitalism to state socialism and back within 50 years during the last century, and for the past 20 years has been practising the most radical form of neoliberal market economy. In many ways the border is not the most favourable place to be. On the other hand, it has provided an understanding of the paradoxically short-term validity of any large-scale agenda. In fact, the fast tactical decisions taken have often forced a rethink of long-term strategies. This is not to say that long-term planning and decision-making are useless, but rather that we are swinging towards the other extreme of the pendulum where long-term forecasts have become increasingly difficult to make. I believe it is not a local phenomenon but a global one; something that first comes to the fore in the most vulnerable settings – on the border.

Ironically, border conditions are to be found in the middle of every discipline, in the midst of all sorts of things where specific forms and specialisations have not yet taken shape, where errors and detours are not taken for mistakes, where the selection of relevant components has not yet been formalised, and where knowledge and skills from other disciplines are welcome in the search for an integral and relevant way forward. Instead of the fixed and well-documented examples at the limits of the profession, these conditions in the middle have been the driving force, the *élan vital*, for the discipline itself and its teaching.

The nature of architectural practice and education has always been essentially transdisciplinary. The difference between then and now is in the scale: in the amount of information it builds on and in the variety of potential outcomes. There are several reasons why this has happened, which have led to a somewhat different setting for contemporary practice and education.

DIFFUSION OF THE PROFESSION

The requirements for practising architecture have increased substantially. The technological sophistication of new buildings and project documentation has risen to an unprecedented level. Partly, this is a technological requirement – it is only natural that the profession is able and willing to integrate the best of the latest technologies – but it is also increasingly an institutional one. Instead of controlling and regulating the quality of practitioners and, accordingly, their access to the market, the liberal economies choose to massively regulate the conditions that the service has to meet. Society traditionally regulates and controls fire protection, sustainability, natural habitats, street and road networks, all communication infrastructures, and also large-scale planning decisions, to name just the main areas, all of which evolve their own ever more complex regulatory mechanisms. In addition, we are now witnessing increasing standardisation of the project itself in all its parts.

Massive regulation has produced the faulty impression that fulfilling the regulations is all there is to a building project. Almost anyone with appropriate knowledge of construction today can compile the necessary documentation, in which all areas of the project are treated according to the regulations – except the design itself, as there are no rules for architectural quality. In the liberal states there has also been a serious decrease in state control over urban planning processes, which has meant the loss of staff, expertise and the power of local planning offices. This creates a situation where the building project can effectively rule out all design questions, and consequently the profession responsible for it. As a paradoxical result (with regard to what are historically the most complex requirements for the project), the profession traditionally responsible for design tends to be less needed.

Architecture as a discipline seems to be too general for the myriad of specific problems that need to be dealt with. Under these unfavourable conditions we see architects becoming highly inventive with respect to their employment possibilities and expanding the profession into less regulated and more short-term areas of practice, such as researching and designing spatial experiences, exhibition concepts, computing, processing, etc. Architectural practice as we used to know it still exists for the few, whereas the architectural field of practice and self-realisation is wider than ever.

DISSOLUTION OF THE PUBLIC

If we look at the current design of public spaces, we are witnessing the identification of, and orientation towards, an increasing number of specific user groups. New parks today have fenced and equipped areas for dogs (sometimes two different ones for dogs of different sizes), fenced and equipped areas for small children, well equipped areas for older children, sportsmen and joggers, skateboarders and roller skaters, clearly defined bicycle routes and more loosely defined areas for picnics, benches, etc. The somewhat simple, modernist terms of street, square and park, unless further elaborated, have lost their appeal and conviction. This user specification is similar to what we see in the development of sports equipment. The simple and straightforward distinction between outdoor and indoor wear of the modernist era sports programme has been long replaced by a spectacular array of highly specific gear for cycling, roller skating, skateboarding, mountain climbing, hiking and running, not to mention the myriad water and winter sports.

The fragmentation of the general modernist "public" has led to the dissolution of the public client. If we try to work for the "public good", who exactly is it for? With the prevailing liberal market economy, the control of planning processes and real estate development has to a large extent moved from states and local governments to private capital. This varies in degree from the extreme neoliberalism of the Baltic countries, especially Estonia during the past two decades, to a much softer shift away from the welfare states in Scandinavia – but the general trend is the same. Within the free market, we tend to find ourselves on our own among a wide field of stakeholders and interest groups, and with little coordination from local governments on more general public agendas.

Private capital, local community, history and environment protection activists, planners and architects are treated as equal players in a simple market operation where the ones with a stronger voice prevail. The dissolution of the public client has left the architect on his own with private capital, which is looking for comparatively cheap labour for the effective spatial and material formalisation of a predetermined financial machine – one in which critical and visionary thinking and quality are not part of the deal. If we cannot participate in the rather complex negotiations and provide new and integral models of intervention, we are left with the simplest of technical jobs in order to fulfil a business plan.

TRANSDISCIPLINARY EDUCATION AND RESEARCH

Under the pressure of increasing specialisation and fragmentation (from both the market and society at large), architectural education is developing in two seemingly opposing directions that eventually tend to contribute to and support each other. On the one hand, education is dispersing into a multitude of different branches – sustainability issues, computing, processing, robotics and material studies, to name just a few very broad categories. On the other, it is concentrating on the formation of complex, hybrid new assemblages, which, besides buildings, now vary from large-scale planning issues to settlement patterns, or digital processing and building solutions. The ever-increasing variety of knowledge and skills necessary for these rather different activities in the architectural field is clearly impossible to teach within the architectural curriculum.

What makes it possible, however, for our graduates to move rather freely in the midst of these very different creative areas, is their designerly understanding about how things are put together, and how to intervene in the existing set of things. Largely, it has been studio work that has trained designer skills, both the mindset to arrange different constituents into new and meaningful wholes, and the parallel, endless tests of the specific spatial and material structures. Besides the studio, transdisciplinary education needs to teach subjects (although in what proportion has been long disputed) in order to be able to communicate with and understand different disciplines and to be able to ask the relevant questions.

Research skills are essential and not so different from design skills – we reach the relevant understanding of a context and acquire the appropriate methodology for a specific situation through experimenting and actual practice. Research in transdisciplinary practice does not easily fall into any of the current taxonomies of education and research: though neither a social or natural science nor an art, architecture needs and uses all of these while producing results of its own. Research here is not about "what is" but about "how it has come about": how and into what it could be changed. We need to be able to understand, and often reinvent, the ways in which we acquire contextual, tacit knowledge and the ways in which we can use it. Research through practice and studio work is itself a powerful tool to help deal with the rapidly changing society, market and profession.

Experimental practice rules out any fixed preconceptions and operates in the field of case-specific decisions. Each project is particular: the conditions have to be defined anew each time. Being in the middle of all that is happening right now might be the only valid position from which our education can still intervene and make a difference; it is an extreme border condition from which anything can emerge, both in terms of individual practice and for the profession as a whole. Architectural education has to become more tactical – again without losing the longer-term and wider perspective. It needs to strengthen its ability to take initiative and make fast and efficient moves in all areas of the field of architecture. Estonia's last 20 years' history of extreme neoliberalism has led to survival mechanisms where the main strategy is "Let's see what we can do" – and there is always a way to intervene, a demand for an architect, which unravels in a myriad of completely unpredictable ways. Education as a mix of curriculum and studio work with well-integrated research needs to provide an ever-broader – transdisciplinary – agenda to remain relevant. The future cannot be invented, but has to be lived and formed continuously.

Toomas Tammis is an architect and currently the Dean of the Faculty of Architecture of the Estonian Academy of Arts. He studied architecture at the Estonian Academy of Arts in Tallinn and the Architectural Association School of Architecture in London and is the founding partner of ArhitektuuriAgentuur and Allianss Arhitektid. He is currently working on establishing a design practice research and PhD programme in the EAA. The most prominent works include a holiday village in Vamråk, Norway (with Paco Ulman), Spa Hotel in Kuressaare, Estonia (with Tarmo Teedumäe and Inga Raukas) and several apartment buildings and private residences in and around Tallinn. ⚏

THE MERIT OF SAUNTERING —

Machiel Spaan

English interpreter, Laura Vroomen

Every now and then there is a general consensus that things have to change, prompted, for example, by the advent of a new technology, a looming energy crisis or an economic recession. Such a key moment, a potential tipping point, is upon us now: the banking crisis, the general malaise across Europe, the huge national surplus of buildings and the stagnated development in various areas. What are architects expected to do in this day and age? What questions should they be asking? What possible approaches are available to them? And how are architecture schools dealing with the current situation, this new reality?

Every now and then someone draws on such a tipping point to develop an original perspective and a cogent plea for regeneration. One such person was the German cultural philosopher Walter Benjamin. In the 1920s and 1930s, a politically, socially and economically turbulent period, Benjamin lived in various European cities. In his unfinished masterpiece *Das Passagen-Werk* (The Arcades Project, 1927–1940), he gives an unusually fragmentary and filmic account of all the facets of the decaying shopping arcades in Paris. [1] Benjamin deconstructs the buildings. He draws up inventories of their structures and details: catacombs, cast-iron constructions, interiors, mirrors, as well as the techniques underlying all of these components. The entire arcade is dissected. Its users are also identified and defined: from *clochards* to commercial traders, from artists to the upper middle classes. And their behaviour is described: the collecting mania, boredom, fashion fads and vanity. But Benjamin also paints a bigger picture. He travels around town, seeing the railways, the Seine, Haussman's Boulevards and the stock exchange. He reads up on the city's history, studies its economy, literature, conspiracies, sects, painting and progress. He tries to get to grips with the overall cultural, political and social situation. *Das Passagen-Werk* is a comprehensive work, an exhaustive collection of fragments, impressions, thoughts and narratives. It contains all the information needed to understand a structure like the Parisian Arcades.

Until recently, the conventional architectural commission had often been a clear-cut assignment based on a particular building plot, a specific programme and predetermined users. These days, an architect's commission is no longer just about the design of buildings, but also increasingly about understanding the city itself, and that includes the urban space, its users and the atmosphere. This new reality is extremely complex. Set against the backdrop of transforming buildings and cities, the commissions defy clear-cut description: both location and context are often undefined and open to multiple interpretations; the potential users may still be unknown and the conceivable future unclear. So before the architect can embark on the actual design of the building, the commission must be set up, defined and formulated. And to do so, the architect must not get too bogged down in the physical site at this early stage, but rise above it in order to broaden his or her perspective, take note of all the constraints and the social conditions, and picture an attractive future. The architect can be a mediator between all of

1. Benjamin, Walter, *The Arcades Project*, Rolf Tiedemann ed, Howard Eiland and Kevin McLaughlin trans, New York: Belknap Press, 2002. Original title: *Das Passagen-Werk*, 1927–1940.

these dimensions in this ambiguous zone in which the design, site and future users come together. Architects give shape to this liminal zone between space, site and use. They map, listen and interpret. This new architect is an intermediary, arriving at a diagnosis and outlining a vision: one which either marks the start of the actual design or, in some cases, renders it unnecessary.

Clear, unbiased thinking has become an essential part of the design commission. Only a proper scrutiny of both context and conditions can lead to the correct hypotheses and a meaningful design. During the mediation phase the architect will have to look freely and observe the city without seeking truth or passing judgement. While doing so, the architect must not jump to conclusions that might bring about hasty or biased solutions. In our current digital world, this will have to be a conscious decision. The media and the Internet inform us so quickly; they create the illusion that it is easy to accelerate the design process. "We understand so quickly that we forget to imagine", wrote Gaston Bachelard in *Air and Dreams*.[2] Imagination is so much more than downloading photos or articles from the Internet and printing them off. "We always think of the imagination as the faculty that forms images. On the contrary, it *deforms* what we perceive; it is, above all, the faculty that frees us from immediate images and changes them. If there is no change, or unexpected fusion of images, there is no imagination [...] There is only perception", Bachelard writes in the introduction to the same essay. Gaining access to this imagination is an essential part of the mediating phase of design. This is where images of the site, user and future will have to fuse into one coherent vision. This fusion will create the foundation for the commission.

2. Bachelard, Gaston, *Air and Dreams: An Essay on the Imagination of Movement*, Edith and Frederick Farrell trans, Dallas: The Dallas Institute Publications, 1988, p 53.

Good architectural training stimulates this imagination in students, giving them the tools to observe, listen, see and interpret. Good education offers students the space to investigate, to explore and to discover. To do this, the classic design commission must be cracked open. The commission is not just about creating a sound building design. In the beginning there is no brief, no location, no programme and no user. There is only the city in all its complexity. This city is the starting point for observation.

John Hejduk, the architect and former director of the renowned Cooper Union School of Art and Architecture, tries to spark imagination in himself and his students as follows: in *Masks* he explores several European cities in a highly personal and painstaking way. His inventories lead to evocative, poetic stories that all offer a unique take on the cities he observes. His stories bare the city's 'soul', prompt dialogue, inspiration, personal thoughts and visionary ideas. "The architect is responsible to create 'the spirit of a thought'. And to translate through whatever medium is available a 'sense of space': whether it be in a text, in a *drawing*, in a model, in a building, in a photograph, or in a film. The architect concerns himself/herself with the mysteries of space and form, and is also obligated to invent new programmes."[3] Hejduk's drawings and poems depict coagulated fragments of the city: parks, residential buildings, cultural spaces, commemorative places, workshops for builders and carpenters, studios for artists. The images have been carefully arranged by Hejduk. Each occupies a specific place within a matrix that tries to encompass all aspects of urban life. Image and text tell a story while at the same time giving the reader plenty of space. Hejduk's *Masks* are not dissimilar from the fragmented texts in Walter Benjamin's *Das Passagen-Werk*. Benjamin calls these forms of imagination *denkbilder*: images that create the necessary space for a personal experience of the city.

3. Hejduk, John, *Berlin Night*, Rotterdam: NAi, 1993.

Walter Benjamin was a philosopher as well as a keen collector, traveller and writer. He collected everything, from picture postcards to catalogues and gadgets. The objects themselves helped him arrive at the most detailed understanding of things. On his travels he met the world. He spoke, argued and

110

learnt. In his writing he dreams of the future, of new technologies making the world a better place. To Walter Benjamin the designer is a *flâneur*. A *flâneur* who is right at the centre of his work environment, who looks around and is not tied to a schedule. A *flâneur* who is always on the move, who experiences all urban processes and keeps viewing them from different perspectives. And so he sees the city from all possible angles, meets everyone and thinks freely and associatively. The *flâneur* does not target a single aspect of the city, but is aware of the relationships between them. This allows him to experience the true dynamic of urban life. The philosopher Frédéric Gros [1] compares the *flâneur* to the hiker: "the hiker thrives on immersing himself in nature. The *flâneur* on losing himself in a succession of thrills".

Gros, Frédéric, *A Philosophy Walking*, John Howe trans, York/London: Verso, 2014.

In the year 2014 the architect is also a collector, traveller and writer. Architects collect all elements of the existing city, street and building. They go in search of peers and talk to them. Architects start by talking, collecting, making, drawing and writing. Building comes last. They will explore potential uses and dream of possible futures using every available tool to transform the present into something new. They appreciate what is found, and combine, embrace, exclude and intervene.

In this day and age, a good school of architecture is no longer a sealed fortress or a monastery. The school has become part of the city, a laboratory for urban complexity. The city is observed, discovered and mapped. School and city merge. Good architectural training embraces the art of sauntering in the midst of society, indefinitely, and without a predetermined design result. It stimulates and develops the imagination cited by Bachelard and Hejduk.

By spending lengthy periods of time roaming the entire city and its liminal zones you can catch a glimpse of the future. Boredom can be a springboard for great achievements. The architect as *flâneur* saunters around the city, attempting to mediate between past times, contemporary images and assignments for a forgotten future.

Machiel Spaan is an architect and co-founder of the Amsterdam-based architecture firm M3H architecten, which devotes attention to all facets of design, from an urban scale to the detail. Making and building are key aspects. In addition to his practice, Machiel Spaan has been actively teaching since 1994. He has focused on creating a sensory experience of architecture in educational projects. Machiel has been head of the Architecture Department at the Amsterdam Academy of Architecture. Important motives are the process of creation, the relation with the arts and the social context.

DESIGN FOR THE MISSING MIDDLE —
ARCHITECTURE IN A CONTEXT OF INEQUALITY

Hannah Le Roux

Our architecture course involves an admission interview. One student – I will call him Thomas – arrived with a sturdy and meticulous model of his dream house, with walls glued together from hundreds of used matchsticks, gutters from spliced drinking straws, and roof flashings made from cold drink cans. He had kept it intact over thirty miles of minibus taxi trips from Orange Farm, a sprawling informal settlement where the average household income is around €100 per month, a place from which we were yet to have a student. Thomas aced his interview, giving quiet and focused responses, and when it was over he insisted that I keep the model.

Thomas, unlike the young hero in a charity campaign, did not make it onto the course and go on to become a licensed architect. He failed the maths exams required for university entrance. He never came back to collect the model, which I kept for a few years until donating it to a crèche. Passing on Thomas' dream house to inspire a new generation was the only way to exorcise the deep sadness that it represented to me, the sense of loss of another generation of young talent, even a decade after Mandela's release.

Young people like Thomas cannot cross the chasm of South Africa's inequality. The vast majority of them fail to obtain that crucial maths mark of 40 per cent that opens the door to a technical degree, often because their own teachers, with limited basic skills, are teaching classes of over 40 pupils. Their situation is amplified by spatial inequality. The persistent topography of apartheid planning, which separated impoverished labour reserves and productive downtowns, makes access to education or jobs unaffordable for the poor.

Over and above the political dangers inherent in such deep and persistent differences, it is the absence of commonality that creates the everyday crisis in education and the economy at large. The so-called missing middle, whether reflected in the sparsity of extra support for poor, gifted youth, or subsidised transport, or mixed income neighbourhoods, is both the problem and the opportunity for transformation.

South Africa has no shortage of practical intelligence within each sector of its divided communities. The poor have evolved extraordinary spatial practices for housing, from the systematic building of backyard shacks to prefabricated corrugated metal wall panels sold on the roadside of any growing settlement. They organise nationwide syndicates for buying cheaper food, have collective saving schemes, produce alternative medicines and run a mass transport system of minibus taxis that was built without any state subsidies. The wealthy, including many whites who left the public service at the end of apartheid, have since become successful entrepreneurs who dominate the African and local markets for mobile telephones, banking services, construction and logistics. South Africans understand mining and nuclear, solar, wind and hydro energy, as well as agriculture and conservation on a large scale.

Yet the practices at both ends of this spectrum are inefficient in their own ways. It is those rare practices that span between them that show the real potentials for growth in its every sense – social, economic and conceptual. As a contribution to the debate, various transformative practices have been explored within education through dialogue and sometimes collaboration with outside agencies. Far from being mainstream, however, the idealism of critical spatial practice often meets with resistance when it proposes alternatives to the status quo of building practices, or, more specifically, contracting processes for state assets. Moreover, there are no agencies that disburse funds for experimental architectural practice as a form of ideas research. This gap places an obligation on the progressive architecture schools to function as places of experimentation, but even within them, alternative practitioners often have to work without support in the funding or implementation of their research.

Despite these constraints and the history of architecture as a practice being defined in relation to wealth, a number of teacher-practitioners strongly believe in the potential for architecture to engage with the creative resources of poor communities as a way of adding economic and social value. Co-designing better schools in partnership with the urban communities of the Cape Flats or making them with local builders and materials in rural areas are immediate examples.[1] The documentation of self-constructed environments and public space, the development of indigenous materials, and the application of landscape design strategies to ameliorate polluted post-mining landscapes are some of these explorations which, if not yet common practice in our schools and young studios, are emerging exponentially.

At Wits, we have experimented with design-build as in the KwaThema project.[2] There is a long tradition of research and design studios in numerous everyday contexts as far back as the 1960s, from Peter Rich's documentation of informal settlements in Alexandra to Melinda Silverman's explorations of small towns,[3] and, lately, the dense transportation and retail cores of the inner city.[4] This tradition of realism has broadened to include other institutions, such as the University of Johannesburg, which, along with the practice 26'10, mixed design, activism and exhibition activities in relation to the warehouses of Marlboro South that have been filled with housing.[5] At UCT, there is valuable work being done that investigates government school buildings in the Cape Flats and proposes alternatives through design.

The costs of such projects are either self-funded by the universities or supported by foreign cultural agencies. While there are numerous conversations with individuals about the possibilities that are imagined in our studios, it is as if we operate in a space of fiction and not in the reality of either the State or the private developers, who are the real producers of new urban interventions at scale. One could argue that the polarised agendas of public agencies which act as welfarist providers of housing and informal settlement upgrades for a voting bloc of poor people, and a private sector that commodifies space for the wealthy away from poverty and crime, both profit from inequality and have no interest in cutting out or creating the middle ground.

Perhaps we need to be more focused in seeking out partners who themselves wish to work towards the definition of mixed economies, and more active in publicising the potential that we recognise in them. Alongside these internal practices, our schools need to engage with visionary individuals in public works and planning departments. In this respect, we should open the modes of engagement between the architecture profession and the state and move away from their legacy of quite secretive practices. The media have untapped potential as a route to presenting designerly visions as a way of influencing policy agencies,

1. In rural practice, see for instance the work of Iain Low with "Building for Self Reliance in the 1980's" in Judin, H, and Vladislaviç, I, *Blank_: architecture, apartheid and after*, Rotterdam: NAi, and at present, by the Austrian NPO, buildcollective, 1998, see http://buildcollective.net/onsite/category/projects/classroom/.

2. In Spitz, R, *HfG IUP IFG: Ulm 1968-2008*, Ulm: Design Forum FG Ulm, 2012.

3. See Silverman, M, ed, *2003–2007. Urban Change in a Small South African Town*, (five volumes). Johannesburg: University of the Witwatersrand.

4. See Jeppe exhibit for "Smart Cities" at the 5th International Architecture Biennale, Rotterdam, curated by Hannah Le Roux with students from the Architecture programme, University of the Witwatersrand, 2012.

5. Le Roux, H, "Marlboro South", *Domus*, 23 May 2013.

where design as a strategy for change is barely understood. There is also a critical role for professional institutions and insightful individuals to use pilot and case studies as examples for leading collective workshops and public engagements. And we need to articulate the histories that brought us to this moment in order to pinpoint what needs to change and what resists it.

But beyond the practical capacities of education, however, we also need to harness its potential for personal border crossings. The self-development implicit in design education and critical thinking needs support in order for it to happen in an open and nuanced way, thus allowing the post-apartheid generation to seek out hybrid identities and identifications. Under the right conditions, our students' experience of otherness is a spark for innovation. How it happens is an open question, but such moments of insight can be glimpsed in a range of situations: in arts-led creative spaces, during collaborative building projects in rural areas, and in travel to places of *mixité*.

One transforming experience for many students of architecture and urbanism has been their visit to Maputo, 600 kilometres away, both a mere hop in Africa and a world apart. In this town, 40 years after independence from Portugal, the middle has been made and unmade enough times through colonial *mixité* and postcolonial contingency to present a far richer urban experience than can be found in Sandton or Soweto. There is also a stronger culture of *making do*, the manifestation of people abandoning the expectation that the state will provide for the poor, and a positive alternative to the protests of South Africans when in fact it does not. With self-build as a ubiquitous practice, Maputo presents an urbanism that is mostly middle ground.

At the time of writing, the urgent need to transform the way we operate in South Africa, both in thinking and practice, has been highlighted by well publicised acts of anger enacted against colonial era statues and African immigrants. The frustration with exclusion and disparity are reaching dangerous levels. Yet it strikes me as unlikely that an aspirant architect like Thomas would be acting out his frustrations over exclusion in this way. What he presented in his dream house was a vision, and certainly a fiction without that maths pass, but one that can be sustaining at a dark time. What his vision in turn represents is that architecture is a concrete narrative that can give a form, materiality and place to something we imagine, beyond the boundaries we inherit.

Hannah Le Roux is Director of Architecture, School of Architecture and Planning, University of the Witwatersrand. ▼

CONFRONTING THE PERMANENT CRISIS —

José María Wilford Nava Townsend

To build, to transform the living space in a perennial search to find a shelter where we can shape our microcosm: the sum of individualities which forms the collective body of what we understand as a society, whether concentrated or dispersed, in conflict or harmony. When did we raise the very nature of what we are to the rank of the sublime? When did we begin to transform our basic need to inhabit and configure our space into a sensitive screening exercise? Consciously or unconsciously, it was when we, as architects, resigned ourselves to confronting what we call our profession as a state of permanent crisis.

In its crisis, architecture may emerge as the unlimited desire of an anonymous community to endure, or as the imposing arrogance of a ruthless tyrant. It extends from the sum of individualities that intertwine to form a whole, to the determined individual who aims to identify an idea, a feeling or a characteristic, stripping it of the blanket that protects its anonymity within the whole.

It is only by chance that I am writing this, while the bus takes me with my current group of students to a destination where there are exquisite examples of architecture and landscape. Along the way, however, we are crossing all the borders of the city of the rich and the poor. The universe of self-construction housing, built with concrete bricks by thousands of souls who need to provide a shelter for their families, creating a landscape of thousands of grey prisms that claim possession of the environment. The city where limited effort is made by the construction professional, in collaboration with the public administration and the real estate developer, to create a ghost of order out of the indiscriminate repetition of a module based on a prejudiced idea of what a home should be. The city of residences of the rich, which form a set of isolated and fortified cloisters, inspired by a fear of everything that surrounds them. And the city of factories, stores, warehouses, and other facilities that feed the system that feeds all of the above. We are travelling on the same edge that connects all the borders and the intersecting space, which, paradoxically, forms an impenetrable barrier to transverse crossing.

While the melancholy of this landscape overwhelms my senses and shakes me as I find an unexpected beauty in the prismatic collectivity of the irregular settlements (the very ones that were forgotten by the divine hand of the architect); while the horrible creative plasticity of attempts to exhibit the wealth of a client (translated into a luxury residence made by hundreds of colleagues and displayed in the fortified enclosures of those who can afford them) begins to produce in me an unsettling intellectual indigestion; and while we pass the endless modular houses that the real estate sprawl designates to mask the failure of a system located on the border (its very own border) of a permanent collapse, I shall prepare a statement that deals with a projected vision about the future of architectural education.

I want to believe, then, that the meaning of architecture as a permanent exercise in crisis management provides a suitable environment for developing alternatives for understanding living space. I want to believe, then, that the complexity and rich variations that manifest the living space will end sooner or later, bringing conformity also to the cultural structures that determine not an era, but the ongoing evolution of a community. I also want to understand that this cultural dimension, which is as wide as cultural diversity itself, is able, at any given moment, to transcend the terrible and sad misconception usually assumed by the elite, that culture is only the limited paraphernalia of exquisite expressions. I believe that architecture serves to build.

As a first approach, we must promote an understanding of the various strategies for occupying space, with its iconic collective references, as well as providing the resources to convert them into building systems which can coexist at the edges that define the different fractions of a collective whole, thus renouncing the messianic determinism of absolute formulas. This should be, in my humble opinion, the initial speech for introducing architecture as a learning process. And from there, we must learn to detect the borders that delimit each social, cultural, economic, environmental and political phenomenon, accepting the various fractions and the conflicts between them as an irrefutable fact of continuity.

At the same time it is also indispensable to identify the different kinds of flows that serve several agglomerations of inhabitants occupying the same living space, and the interactions that occur between them. Scale has become relative, and so have some of the traditional words used to name certain contexts. Some cities have more inhabitants than many countries, there are buildings that have more inhabitants than some cities; houses exist that are smaller than objects considered as urban furniture. Can we really define as "urban" the dynamics of flows of a town with 50,000 inhabitants, and as "architectural" those of a building containing the same number of people? What happens to the dynamics of flows of a purely rural municipality, which also contains 50,000 inhabitants? What other living species affect or are affected by the dynamics produced by human flows in each case? We have to consider living space as a constantly moving organism, and therefore conceptualise building not as a static result of a construction process, but as a temporal shape that will be transformed by its users and their flow necessities in the course of time.

A desirable direction for new ways of composition would be to recover the ability to understand building systems and their capacities, and the possibility of generating new alternatives by mixing different systems into new ones in a permanent process of experimentation, exercising design methodologies as tools to elaborate the connection between the necessities of the living space, its flows in relation to the specific context, and the possibilities of an adequate building system.

However, here in Mexico at least, the global economic crisis has led to a negative impact on students' expectations regarding their contribution as professionals to the future of society. This is not the natural generation gap that normally exists between "the young and the restless" and "the old, experienced and established", but resembles more of an unsettling feeling that there is no more hope in finding a common path. It is the feeling that professions and their academic apparatus are an obsolete scheme absorbed in an expanding process of accumulating professional degrees. These are not a comfort anymore; they are gained through a cloistered experience and demand a transformation through practical activities.

What should be done to revert this feeling of impotence? How do we capture the sparkle that will reinvent the role of the architect in a transforming ecosystem? How can we transmit that sparkle to the new generations of architects?

All of the elements I mentioned earlier are fundamental but irrelevant if we are not able to find the essence that gives birth to every construction, every building. It is the essence which, if captured, will give sense to everything we do.

We are already trying to understand the complexity of living and building through a wider and more scientific approach (and we should develop and improve these methodologies). We are already investigating human activities and behaviours individually and socially to comprehend the effects that these have on the transformation of the living space (let's keep going). We now know that the whole system needs to be reconfigured in a sustainable equilibrium, and so sustainable architecture has to be understood as a critical approach to the way we interact with a place as part of it, and not just a fancy way to wear clever accessories. We have understood that it is time for schools of architecture and their institutions to use real places with real problems as the best laboratory to work in, and we have opened our cloisters to interact in our academic work with real communities that otherwise cannot afford to obtain an architectural consultant. All of these aspects, and many more besides, have already changed the way architecture is taught and practised compared with the past. Why, then, do I have the feeling that something is missing?

As I am on the road with my students, returning from the field trip we made to study and learn from the Hidalgo State Mining haciendas of the eighteenth century and the impact they had at that time – how they transformed the people's way of life in that region (for better or worse), and the spectacular architecture they represent – we are once again crossing all the borders of the contemporary city, my Mexico City, the place where I was born. As I see again all the constructions I described before, I realise the common link between them, the essence behind every construction, no matter the era, ideology, economical system or sociological status under which they were made. No matter if they are the manifestations of a migratory phenomenon or a process of local development.

That essence is hope... for something, for everything.... Hope for sustaining life as a foundation sustains a building. My favourite definition of architecture used to be Le Corbusier's "Architecture is the learned game, correct and magnificent, of forms assembled in the light." But today, as I conclude this statement, I shall say that architecture is the space that provides a home for the spark of hope. All the techniques, all the scientific methodologies, all the different approaches, all the understanding of culture, borders and sustainable needs are useless if we cannot transmit to our students, and to the future users of their architecture, the essence of a spark of hope.

José María Wilford Nava Townsend is full-time professor and researcher at the Universidad Iberoamericana, in the fields of Architecture and Urban Development, and coordinator of the Architecture 5-year Bachelor programme at the Universidad Iberoamericana. He is an associate of the private practice architecture firm Obra Gris in partnership with architects María del Carmen Freyre Martínez, Paola Peralta Horta and Gilda Lara Quintana.

ENGAGEMENT AND ARCHITECTURE —
REFLECTIONS ON A PROFESSIONAL MID-LIFE CRISIS

Micha de Haas

What is the relevancy of an expressive skyline for society? Who cares if a building corner is transparent or not? Why on earth does it really matter if a window frame is detailed in timber or aluminium? Does it even slightly improve the wellbeing of the user? Does it really have any effect on a community beyond the sheer aesthetic experience?

No architect would voluntarily admit to it, but after years of practice you might stare one morning at the computer screen or sketch roll and realise that you are in the midst of a professional mid-life crisis.

A healthy wake-up call, which is indeed essential for the vitality of the profession, since we should time and again ask ourselves a fundamental question: what is our basic motivation for producing architecture?

As architecture students, most of us encountered the ethos of the enlightened yet completely self-centred architect. Brunelleschi, for instance, was so enraged by the presumed ignorance of his Florentine clients that he had to be forcefully removed from the council meeting, exclaiming in the process that he was the sole professional capable of properly vaulting their cathedral. And indeed later, as Vasari tells us in his *Lives of the Artists*, the council approached the master again in his atelier, begging him to resume the commission – which, of course, he haughtily agreed to do.

Another example is Ayn Rand's protagonist in her novel *The Fountainhead*, a book that for all the wrong reasons has inspired the career choice of a whole generation of architects. The uncompromising Howard Roark – the ideal representation of Rand's revered individualism – chooses to detonate his major building project because the client insists on some adjustments.

In the same period it was argued passionately that architecture is a tool to mould life and society, a way to facilitate social justice and even more: that creating the right spatial environment brings out the best in peoples' behaviour.

It seems that these two seemingly contradictory insights actually justified each other: because we *know* that our buildings will change society, we feel we have every right to force everyone to submit to our superior spatial creations – an attitude that for a long period of time shaped both the public image and the self-image of contemporary architects.

Should architecture idealise self-expression or social commitment? We need to elaborate and reflect on these two positions at more length.

Why do we make design decisions? "Because I like it" is a common, almost banal response from students during studio sessions. We could ridicule it and render it premature, but looking at the harvest in many architectural magazines, it seems as though this is a fundamental sentiment in the professional community. Following this line, architecture is a self-referential discipline which can only be judged and discussed on the basis of architectural arguments, be they spatial, logistical, technical or aesthetic. But are we indeed producing designs exclusively within the semi-autistic context of an architectural discourse?

Fortunately, numerous others argue that architecture should be discussed in a broader, inclusive context: the city, our society, the global environment, politics, etc. The inevitable foundation for this approach is the conviction that the architect's basic motivation is synonymous with a word which has become so politically correct it is almost hard to pronounce it without cynicism, or at least an apologetic smile: engagement.

From a historical perspective, the modern movement in architecture was probably the first of its kind to be seriously engaged in social and ethical discussions. The Van Nelle factory, for example, was inspired by the need to create better working conditions for the employees. Mart Stam, Ernst May and other architects moved to the Soviet Union at the beginning of the twentieth century in order to design cities that were meant to create the conditions for a new social utopia. Yet the fact that these cities were later heavily criticised as inhuman, demonstrates that engagement and idealism alone do not guarantee good architecture or urbanism.

One should not be tempted to link engagement in architecture mainly to the political left or to ethics. In the 1940s, Nazi architects designed the Prora on the island of Rugen as a free vacation resort for German workers, a fantastic social idea, cast in modern architecture yet rooted in racial theory. Another known episode features Le Corbusier, who in his eagerness to realise his urban social utopia, *Ville Radieuse*, turned to the pro-Nazi Vichy government and pleaded for this enlightened regime to "do the right thing" and build it. In Israel, ideologically motivated architects and planners are designing settlements that, aside from providing housing, are also intended to create a *fait accompli* in the sensitive geopolitical status quo of the region.

Engagement is thus not always ethically motivated: the result (ie the architectural object, and not the social change) apparently justifies the means.

Robert van 't Hoff, a promising architect who was extremely involved in the social and political movement of his time, bitterly abandoned the profession (and destroyed most of his archive) in 1945, disillusioned by the absence of any positive social change or effect it had had. An interesting detail is that both the socialist Van 't Hoff and the right-wing rationalist Rand were inspired by Frank Lloyd Wright, who in fact was rather apolitical in his work.

Was Van 't Hoff's disillusion a symptom of a professional mid-life crisis, or was it the result of the profound failure of ideologically motivated architecture? Maybe architecture as a self-referential discipline would not be so bad after all? Maybe this is the only realistic, pragmatic alternative?

During the 1980s, after decades of modernist domination, architects like Philip Johnson adopted a postmodernist position which considered ethics as irrelevant to architecture. A part of this professional community took up typological studies and historicism as the main reference and source of inspiration for design. Other architects immersed themselves in the unprecedented opportunities that technological development was creating for architectural expression. For architecture as a discipline, this was a highly productive and innovative period, which saw the development of new tools and methods for architectural design and building techniques. From an ethical point of view, this period could be labelled "opportunistic".

Aside from its innovative merit, parametric design, for example, can be seen as a way of escaping any form of personal or social responsibility. The aesthetic and technological decadence manifested by the contemporary architecture of, say, the Gulf States and China, is a striking example of its commercial success – on the threshold of a global economic recession. In fact, according to public opinion this architectural *tour de force* is the best representation of the economic frenzy that perpetuated this crisis.

Yet this very crisis was also the starting point for a genuine reflective "soul-searching" process within the profession. Inspired and empowered by the emerging notions of open source, shared knowledge and transparency (with WikiLeaks as its extreme example), and by the borderless accessibility of data and social media, engagement once again became relevant to the architectural discourse.

It is not by chance that architects are starting to play an important role in political activism worldwide. In Turkey, young architects were at the core of the protests over Taksim Park, 2013, which concerned the issue of reclaiming the urban public domain. In Israel, Bimkom (www.bimkom.org.il), a human rights platform of planners and architects, critically addresses the use of spatial planning as a tool of repression. In South America, architects like Alfredo Brillembourg and Hubert Klumpner are producing projects based on participation and "social design" that are receiving worldwide recognition.

Each crisis, a determinist would claim, has its hidden purpose. One could, as the result of a mid-life crisis, buy a sports car or a motorcycle; other people reinvent themselves. Reflecting on the past years of the profession, especially regarding the true value of what has been achieved culturally, economically and socially, can be very confronting. It can, however, also be the source of new insights and choices. Van 't Hoff went on a long solitary walking trip through Europe; Adolfo Natalini traded the early radical ideas of his Superstudio for postmodernist commercialism. These days it seems that some architects are trading cynicism and self-referential decadence for a new kind of engagement.

This new engagement is not based on an ideological programme or a utopian vision. It is a revolt against apathy and is refreshing in its self-conscious activism. It does not require the destruction of the past, a *tabula rasa* or burned bridges in order to manifest itself. It embraces history and the collective memory of the city. It is an architecture that bases its design process on dialogue and participation, and, unlike the social movements in architecture during the 1960s and 1970s, combines pragmatism and solidarity without being naive. One of its most important aspects is the understanding that the notion of engagement should be shared and developed together with clients and users, and be recognised as a form of value creation. It advocates architecture that is, in the first place, process-oriented and only secondarily object-oriented.

From a traditional architectural standpoint one might wonder if this is not a counterproductive development – sacrificing the notion of professional independence to an open source system in which knowledge and professionalism are constantly being relativised; trading the discipline's commitment to excellence in exchange for harvesting as many "likes" as possible.

And doesn't this process-oriented, participation-based approach in fact advocate the irrelevancy of the architectural object? Can this post-cynical architecture produce the spatial qualities and beauty that we all recognise in the Duomo of Florence, the Sagrada Familia church, the Barcelona pavilion, CCTV Beijing or other highlights of self-referential architecture?

Time will tell, but I would argue that even though we like to believe that these magnificent architectural objects are the creation of a single, rigorous creative mind, their designs, too, are the result of an interactive process. A traditional, hierarchic, and linear process indeed, yet the result is still a synthesis.

The change that can be observed these days is an alteration in the process, not in the creative forces. Architectural quality is therefore not inevitably endangered. The architect is still present. His role, however, is no longer to be the personification of his designs; his role, at least as crucial, is to recognise the evident and potential qualities through the (open) process, and *negotiate* them into the design. In contemporary management terms, one can say that the (engaged) architect is actually *coaching* the design.

This changing role creates new responsibilities for the practising architect and new challenges for architectural education. Directed towards a new relevancy for making architecture.

Following his studies at the Bezalel Academy in Jerusalem and the Delft University of Technology, Micha de Haas established his own office in 1997. From the realisation of The Aluminium Forest Knowledge Centre (Houten, 2001), his work has been widely published and has received several awards and nominations. He currently teaches at the Academy of Architecture in Amsterdam and at Delft University of Technology. ▼

ACKNOWLEDGEMENTS —

This publication was initiated and developed by the Border Conditions & Territories research group and financially supported by the Faculty of Architecture (Delft University of Technology), Artifice books on architecture and the Border Conditions Foundation (www.borderconditions.org).

As is common to any publication of this format and size, this book required the involvement of a large group of dedicated editors, authors, scholars, experts, professionals, publishers and other highly engaged professionals who cherish the patience as well as the much anticipated mental and physical 'space' for extended discussions, clarification of details, and the coming to fruit of clear and profound positions and arguments. The editors, Loed Stolte, Oscar Rommens and Marc Schoonderbeek, would like to express their appreciation and gratitude to: DUT-BK deans Professor Karin Laglas and Professor Peter Russell for moral, financial and organisational support; Professor Michiel Riedijk, for his continuous support of the Border Conditions & Territories programme; the authors of the publication, in alphabetical order: Pnina Avidar, Henriette Bier, Marcos Cruz, Martine De Maeseneer, Manuel Gausa, Micha de Haas, Urs Hirschberg, Marc Koehler, Sang Lee, Hannah Le Roux, Sarah Lorenzen, Leonel Moura, Christopher Platt, Javier Quintana, Michiel Riedijk, François Roche, Patrik Schumacher, Malkit Shoshan, Machiel Spaan, Toomas Tammis, José María Wilford Nava Townsend, Gijs Wallis de Vries, Alexander Wright, Alejandro Zaera-Polo, Gerard van Zeijl and Weimin Zhuang; all speakers at the *X Agendas for Architecture* symposium in 2011, respectively Finbarr McComb, Ninke Happel, Max Rink, Hieke Bakker, Petra Pferdmenges, Sander van Schaik, Tom Avermaete, François Roche, Patrik Schumacher, Martine De Maeseneer and Deborah Hauptmann; all lecturers from the *X Agendas for Architecture* Capita Selecta lecture series of 2011 – Sang Lee, Lonn Combs, Patrick Teuffel, Stefano Milani, Marco Frascari, Gerard van Zeijl, Micha de Haas, Malkit Shoshan, Robert-Jan van Pelt, Henriette Bier, Leonel Maura and Marta Malé-Alemany; copyeditor Patricia Brigid Garvin, who meticulously helped in clarifying, correcting and improving all texts; Pnina Avidar, Tom Avermaete, Nadine De Ripainsel and Rui Wang, for dean search assistance and advice; English interpreters Camille Lacadée, Edward A Derbyshire and Laura Vroomen, for careful translations; graphic designer Rachel Pfleger, for being patient with us and still producing a wonderfully designed book; at Artifice books on architecture – Duncan McCorquodale, Kate Trant, Hannah Newell, James Brown, Lauren Whelan and John Bloomfield; San Dino Arcilla and Anna Golubovska, for assistance and clarification at various stages; Bob Somol, for picking up on the Agenda theme for the Chicago Architecture Biennale of 2015.

We would like to dedicate this book to the wonderful memories of: Marco Frascari, who passed in June 2013 and whose influence on the discourse of architecture in general and scholarly work on architectural drawing cannot and should never be underestimated; and Emilie Meaud, Border Conditions alumna and unfortunate victim of the Paris terrorist attacks of November 2015, whose passion for architecture will prevail.

© 2016 Artifice books on architecture, the editors and the authors.
All rights reserved.

Artifice books on architecture
10A Acton Street
London
WC1X 9NG

t. +44 (0)207 713 5097
f. +44 (0)207 713 8682
sales@artificebooksonline.com
www.artificebooksonline.com

All opinions expressed within this publication are those of the authors and not
necessarily of the publisher.

Designed by Rachel Pfleger at Artifice books on architecture.
Edited by Marc Schoonderbeek, Oscar Rommens and Loed Stolte at the Faculty of
Architecture (Delft University of Technology). Copyedited by Patricia Brigid Garvin.
Translations by Camille Lacadée, Edward A Derbyshire and Laura Vroomen.

British Library Cataloguing-in-Publication Data.
A CIP record for this book is available from the British Library.

ISBN 978 1 908967 76 3

Artifice books on architecture is an environmentally responsible company.
X Agendas for Architecture is printed on sustainably sourced paper.